AIR VANGUARD 14

MIKOYAN-GUREVICH MiG-21

ALEXANDER MLADENOV

First published in Great Britain in 2014 by Osprey Publishing,
PO Box 883, Oxford, OX1 9PL, UK
PO Box 3985, New York, NY 10185-3985, USA
E-mail: info@ospreypublishing.com

Osprey Publishing is part of the Osprey Group

A CIP catalogue record for this book is available from the British Library

Print ISBN: 978 1 78200 374 8
PDF ebook ISBN: 978 1 78200 375 5
ePub ebook ISBN: 978 1 78200 376 2

Index by Zoe Ross
Typeset in Sabon
Originated by PDQ Media, Bungay, UK
Printed in China through Asia Pacific Offset Ltd

14 15 16 17 18   10 9 8 7 6 5 4 3 2 1

Osprey Publishing is supporting the Woodland Trust, the UK's leading
woodland conservation charity, by funding the dedication of trees.

www.ospreypublishing.com

CONTENTS

MIKOYAN-GUREVICH MiG-21

INTRODUCTION

The MiG-21 (NATO reporting name: Fishbed) is one of the greatest aircraft of all time, firmly holding the title of the most widely used and widely operated post-war jet fighter, serving with no fewer than 50 air arms worldwide. Originally designed as a faster and lighter successor to the twin-engine/swept-wing MiG-19 (NATO reporting name: Farmer), it pioneered the concept of a single-engine lightweight and speedy tactical jet with a bare minimum of armament, designed to intercept subsonic and supersonic high-altitude bombers, fighter-bombers and cruise missiles in clear-weather conditions.

The chief reason for the MiG-21's success was the basic design's efficient performance, plus the aircraft's simplicity, reliability and affordability. The MiG-21's attributes and sales eventually established the rapidly progressing Moscow-based aircraft design bureau, founded by Artem Mikoyan and Mikhail Gurevich, as the most important fighter design house in the Soviet Union, and it retained this prestigious status until the early 1990s.

The MiG-21's simple low-drag airframe design, conceived already at the time in 1953, was suitably combined with a lightweight and powerful afterburning turbojet, much better and more reliable than the two engines powering its MiG-19 predecessor, coupled with an all-new tailed delta-wing layout with a relatively high wing loading and a small cross-section fuselage. The successful design, featuring low structural weight and low wave drag, offered levels of performance that were very impressive for the second half of the 1950s. High performance in terms of maximum level speed, transonic/supersonic acceleration, rate of climb and service ceiling were deemed essential for the new-style restricted-manoeuvrability air combats with high-speed opponents, expected to be the prime adversaries in the coming decades. The all-new air combat concept in the Soviet Union in the 1950s called for fighter aircraft to follow an optimum intercept flight path and mount a single fast attack pass, during which the aircraft would launch guided missiles in salvo or fire the guns (often provided with a limited number of rounds), followed by immediate breakaway.

The MiG-19 was the first supersonic fighter produced by the Mikoyan & Gurevich Design Bureau, but the type suffered from poor reliability and had a relatively short service career compared to its predecessor the MiG-17 and its successor the MiG-21. (Author's collection)

The Korean War-style high-G turning dogfight between subsonic jet fighters was considered to have been consigned to the history books. Operating in this way, the new-generation high-performance tactical fighter or point-defence interceptor, with an endurance of little over 30 minutes, was expected to be employed *en masse* and capable of rapid take-off for the quick interception of nuclear-armed bombers and fighter-bombers.

As a small and affordable Mach 2/point-defence interceptor, the MiG-21F-13/PF/PFM had no direct equivalents in the Western world in the late 1950s and early 1960s; so in addition to service with the Soviet Union and its allies, the type proliferated in the air forces of a good many non-aligned nations. Its subsequent tactical fighter derivatives, built in the late 1960s and the early 1970s, were considered better suited for low-altitude operations, such as those in the Middle East, than earlier versions. Both the MiG-21MF and MiG-21bis were built and exported in huge numbers in the 1970s and the early 1980s, despite the availability of more modern Soviet fighters cleared for export, such as the MiG-23MS/MF/ML. The latest MiG-21 versions have introduced better armament and expanded air combat and ground-attack capabilities, while still retaining the key advantages of simplicity and affordability. As a consequence, the omnipresent Fishbed continues to be one of the principal fighters in the world's arsenal.

Design bureau founder, Artem Mikoyan. (Mikoyan & Gurevich Design Bureau via author)

DESIGN AND DEVELOPMENT

The sharply-swept vs. delta-wing planform dilemma

The Ye-series of lightweight fighter prototypes, developed in the mid-1950s, were used to good effect in order to evaluate a variety of novel design features intended for the MiG-19's successor. The new fighter was conceived as a lightweight machine, capable of flying much faster and higher than its predecessor. To meet these requirements, the ultimate aim of the Mikoyan & Gurevich Design Bureau, then officially known as OKB-155 (Experimental Design Bureau No. 155), was to develop a simple, single-engine tactical fighter powered by the recently developed Mikulin AM-11 turbojet (later redesignated as the R-11-300), developing 49.05kN (11,000lb st) of thrust in afterburner mode. Development work on the MiG-19's successor commenced following the relevant resolution of the Soviet Council of Ministers, dated 9 September 1953, which authorized development funding and set out the performance targets to be achieved by the design bureau.

Two alternative wing shapes were evaluated during the project definition phase for the new fighter. The first of these was a tapered swept wing with a swept angle of 55°, the same as that of the MiG-19, while the second one called for a delta-wing planform with a leading-edge angle of 57° and conventional horizontal tail surfaces. The swept-wing prototype was designated as the Ye-2, while the delta-wing prototype was initially designated as the Ye-1, but later Ye-4.

Design work on the delta-wing prototype commenced in September 1953, immediately after receiving the relevant authorization from the Soviet government and the Ministry of Aviation Industry, which requested that the aircraft be submitted for its state flight-testing effort in March 1955. The Ye-1 was required to accelerate to no less than 1,750km/h with the engine in afterburner mode for 5 minutes at 10,000m (32,800ft); this altitude was to be

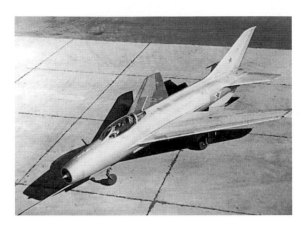

The Ye-2 was a swept-wing prototype, sporting a wing similar to that of the MiG-19 with a swept angle of 55°. (Mikoyan & Gurevich Design Bureau via author)

climbed to in 1.2 minutes and the practical ceiling was set at 18,000–19,000m (59,000–62,300ft). Range requirements called for 1,800km and 2,700km at 15,000m (49,200ft), with and without afterburning respectively, while take-off run and landing-roll requirements called for up to 400m and 700m respectively.

The new fighter was also required to be capable of operating from unpaved runways and performing a constant-speed vertical dive with airbrakes deployed. Its armament suite was set to include three NR-30 30mm cannon aimed via an optical sight coupled to a radar rangefinder, installed inside the nose cone, plus 16 air-to-air rockets in two packs suspended on underwing pylons. This rather unimpressive armament was originally optimized for use against non-manoeuvring bombers, allowing for a single attack run only. Furthermore, during the fighter's design phase, in order to save weight, one of the three NR-30 cannon was deleted.

The difficulties associated with the then new and unknown delta-wing planform delayed the development work, and so priority was given to the prototype featuring the swept-wing planform. This wing configuration was well known at the time in the Soviet Union and the swept-wing prototype design effort at OKB-155 was completed during early 1954, albeit without the new R-11-300 turbojet, developed by the engine design bureau led by A. Mikulin and initially known as the AM-11, due to its considerably delayed development. As a stopgap measure, undertaken in order to speed up the flight testing, the Ye-2 prototype was initially powered by the existing AM-9B engine originally used to power the MiG-19, rated at 31.88kN (7,165lb st) with afterburner.

The Ye-2's wing design closely resembled that of the MiG-19, mounted slightly below mid-position, with an anhedral of -3°. In order to improve the take-off and landing performance, the outer sections of the wings were provided with two-part slats and slotted flaps, while two large aerodynamic strakes were mounted obliquely under the rear fuselage. Later on, in order to avoid the aileron reversal phenomena, the wing was provided with spoilers for roll control. The circular nose air inlet featured rounded lips, intended to create additional sucking force. The prototype's armament included two NR-30 cannon and two eight-round packs of ARS-57 57mm rockets. Aiming both the cannon and the rockets was performed by using the ASP-5N gunsight. The Ye-2 was also designed to use 250kg or 500kg bombs, carried on two hardpoints under the wings, replacing the rocket packs. The swept-wing Ye-2, powered by the interim AM-9B (RD-9B) turbojet, made its maiden flight on 14 February 1954 in the capable hands of OKB-155 test pilot Georgii Mosolov. The first swept-wing prototype, powered by the new R-11-300 turbojet and designated as the Ye-2A/1, was, in fact, a reworked Ye-2. It had waited for one year for its new engine and introduced prominent fences across the wing upper surface.

The Ye-2A/1 made its maiden flight on 17 February 1956 in the hands of OKB-155 test pilot Grigorii Sedov. The initial flight-testing phase proved to be quite difficult due to many teething problems, mainly caused by design deficiencies in both the flight-control system (found to be oversensitive in the roll axis at high indicated speeds) and the brand-new and still immature engine; this eventually caused some 11 months of accumulated grounding time during the flight-testing phase, due to the need to fix the numerous defects

MIXED-POWER YE-50 FOR HIGH-ALTITUDE INTERCEPTIONS

The Ye-50 rocket-boosted fighter-interceptor was a follow-on development based on the Ye-2 design. Work on this mixed-power fighter started at OKB-155 following the resolution of the Council of Ministers dated 19 March 1954 and the subsequent Ministry of Aviation Industry order issued on 24 March 1954. The Ye-50's chief purpose was to intercept free-floating reconnaissance aerostats at altitudes above 25,000m (82,000ft). Such targets were otherwise untouchable for conventional turbojet-powered fighters, which at the time could reach targets flying up to 20,000m (65,600ft).

The mixed-power Ye-50 was to be powered by the AM-11 turbojet and the S-155 two-stage rocket engine; the first stage of the latter was rated at 15.70kN (3,520lb st) and the second stage at 78kN (17,920lb st) at sea level, while at 10,000m (32,800ft) the S-155 developed 19,62kN (4,400lb st) and 39.24kN (8,800lb st) respectively. The rocket engine was intended to be used only during the terminal intercept phase, accelerating the aircraft and enabling it to climb in order to get into the attack position, with the target in sight, and fire its cannon. The S-155 engine was housed inside a fireproof compartment located at the base of the fin. It burned kerosene, using concentrated nitric acid as an oxidizer, while high-test hydrogen peroxide was used to drive the engine's turbine pump unit. The Ye-50's first prototype, designated the Ye-50/1 and powered by the interim AM-9Ye turbojet, made its maiden flight on 9 January 1956 in the hands of OKB-155's test pilot Vladimir Mukhin. Using its rocket engine, the Ye-50/1 demonstrated a maximum speed of 2,470km/h at 18,000m (59,000ft), corresponding to Mach 2.32, while the dynamic ceiling – the maximum ceiling following a ballistic flightpath – was 25,580m (83,900ft). Using the rocket engine's second and more powerful stage, the Ye-50/1 maintained level flight at 20,000m (65,600ft) for 3.1 minutes and while employing the first stage with reduced fuel consumption, the time was extended to 16.2 minutes. The Ye-50/1 had a brief existence, as it was lost on its 18th flight on 14 July 1956 due to a hard landing before the runway threshold following

a mid-air engine failure. Upon impact the aircraft sustained damage beyond repair, but luckily the pilot survived the crash without any significant injures. The second prototype, the Ye-50/2, also powered by the interim RD-9Ye turbojet, featured a number of design improvements; it took to the air for the first time in December 1956 and its flight testing continued until January 1958. The third prototype, designated as the Ye-50/3, was the first to feature built-in armament, represented by two NR-23 23mm cannon. Its internal fuel capacity was increased by some 104 litres, and it featured an extended air inlet with sharpened lips. The Ye-50/3 successfully passed its factory testing phase, but during the acceptance flight for the state testing phase on 8 August 1957 it crashed, killing the NII-VVS test pilot Nikolai Korovin. The root cause of the crash was attributed to an explosion of leaking oxidizer in flight, which, in turn, damaged the flight-control system and the aircraft entered a spin. After realizing that it was impossible to recover the Ye-50/3 in normal flight, Korovin bailed out at low altitude, but his ejection seat malfunctioned; as a result, Korovin fell to the ground still attached to the seat and was killed instantly upon impact.

The Ye-50A was the fourth mixed-power prototype, based on the Ye-2/A airframe and the first one to be powered by the definitive AM-11 engine; it also featured a newly added ventral tank for the oxidizer and the pump assembly. The Ye-50A was expected to offer better performance than its predecessor, with a dynamic ceiling up to 27,200m (89,216ft). It was built in the autumn of 1957, but in February 1959 the State Committee on Aviation Technology (GKAT, established in 1957 as the successor to the disbanded Ministry of Aviation Industry) issued an order to terminate the Ye-50A programme, as all the efforts at OKB-155 were to be focused on completing the MiG-21F and MiG-21P development work. In fact, five series-standard Ye-50As were built at GAZ-21 in Gorkii before termination of the programme; additionally, two aircraft were left in final assembly stage and fuselage parts for eight more were in the process of manufacture.

ABOVE The Ye-50 was a mixed-power interceptor with a swept wing, intended to reach targets at altitudes above 2,000m (6,600ft). Here the second prototype, designated as the Ye-50/2, is shown. (Mikoyan & Gurevich Design Bureau via author)

The Ye-4 prototype introduced an all-new delta wing with a perfect-triangle planform. (Mikoyan & Gurevich Design Bureau via author)

and rectify the malfunctions discovered on the ground and in flight. The second R-11-300-powered prototype, the Ye-2A/2, was flown in June 1956; in December the same year it was submitted for state flight testing, undertaken by the Soviet Air Force's Scientific-Research Institute (NII-VVS) at Akhtubinsk. In 1956 and 1957 this aircraft logged 107 flights, while the Ye-2A/1 added 58 more flights, in order to explore the main flight characteristics. The swept-wing Ye-2A had a take-off weight of 6,250kg and demonstrated a maximum speed of 1,950km/h, corresponding to Mach 1.78, while the practical ceiling was 18,000m (59,000ft), time to 10,000m (32,800ft) was 1.3 minutes and the range reached 2,000km. The two Ye-2A prototypes were grounded after completion of the flight-test programme in 1957, while GAZ-21 (State Aviation Plant No. 21) at Gorkii (now known as Nizhnii Novgorod) commenced production of a five-strong pre-production batch. The new swept-wing fighter was given the series production designation MiG-23.

Delta-wing Ye-4

The prototype with the delta-wing planform was designated as the Ye-4, and its general design concept was presented for the first time in April 1954. As was the case with its swept-wing predecessors, the Ye-2 and Ye-50, the delta-wing prototype began its flight-test programme powered by the interim RD-9B engine in an effort to speed up the definition of the flight characteristics and explore the specific features of the then all-new and still unknown planform. The Ye-4 featured a perfect-triangle planform with pointed wingtips, a span of 7.749m, tracked slotted flaps and one-piece ailerons. The circular nose air inlet had sharp lips and the armament in the beginning comprised three NR-30 30mm cannon, although in the course of the flight-testing effort one of these was removed. Other design alterations undertaken during the Ye-4's flight-test phase included the addition of fences on the wing – initially, two full-chord fences on the underside, but later replaced by three shallower fences, added across the upper surfaces. The delta-wing prototype also received the more powerful RD-9I engine.

The first Ye-4 made its maiden flight on 16 June 1955 with Grigorii Sedov at the controls, and its so-called factory testing phase, undertaken by OKB-155 without NII-VVS involvement, continued until 20 September 1956. The performance demonstrated during these early tests, comprising of 107 flights, proved to be rather disappointing, however, with a maximum speed of only 1,290km/h and a service ceiling of 16,400m (53,800ft). Nevertheless, the Ye-4 proved to be a valuable flying testbed that was used to study the specific features of the then little-known delta-wing planform.

Ye-5 enters flight testing

The Ye-5 was a follow-on delta-wing prototype based on the Ye-4's fuselage and wings, powered by the long-awaited R-11-300 turbojet rated at between 51.99kN (11,660lb st) and 53.96kN (12,100lb st) with afterburning, while the internal fuel capacity was 1,570 litres. In the beginning, the Ye-5 received three aerodynamic fences across the upper surface of each wing, which improved stability in the roll axis at high angle of attack (AoA) and also increased the roll rate. The rear fuselage was shortened and featured an altered shape compared to that of the Ye-4 in a bid to reduce drag. The added fixed tailplane roots were provided with cooling inlets for the engine bay.

Design work on the new prototype at OKB-155 began after the Council of Ministers decree dated 28 March 1956, which required a delta-wing fighter capable of reaching 1,700–1,750km/h maximum speed and 17,000–18,000m (55,800–59,000ft) practical ceiling. Maximum range was to be 1,500km without a drop tank and 2,000km with a drop tank, and the time to 10,000m (32,800ft) was to be within 1.7 minutes. The take-off run was to be less than 400m and the landing roll less than 700m. Armament in the air-to-air mode was to include three NR-30 cannon and two 16-round 57mm rocket packs.

The first example of the Ye-5, designated as the Ye-5/1, was flown for the first time on 9 January 1956 by the OKB-155 test pilot Vladimir Nefyedov; one year later the aircraft received its in-service designation – MiG-21. The more powerful engine – combined with a host of fuselage refinements to improve the aerodynamic performance (mainly for reducing drag) – resulted in a considerably increased maximum level speed, which even exceeded the designer's expectations. On 19 May 1956 the Ye-5/1 reached 1,960km/h maximum speed, corresponding to Mach 1.85 at 11,000m (36,100ft).

In November 1956 the Ye-5/1 was modified, receiving a 400mm fuselage plug on the removable rear fuselage section, shortened ailerons and clipped wingtips in order to improve the aerodynamic performance further, especially the spin characteristics, which were very poor in the beginning. In addition, the fuel capacity was increased to 1,810 litres. After the modifications, the revised Ye-5/1 flew for the first time in February 1957. By May 1958 it had amassed some 98 test sorties, reaching Mach 1.85 at 18,000m (59,000ft). The first pre-production batch of five MiG-21s was built at GAZ-31 in Tbilisi in 1957, and five more examples were reported to be in their final assembly phase by the year's end.

Comparison of the flight performance demonstrated by the Ye-2 and Ye-5 showed that the delta-wing planform of the latter offered lighter structural weight, greater internal fuel capacity and notably better performance in terms of roll rate, turn radius and marginally increased maximum speed. These important points eventually contributed to the Ye-5's selection for serial production.

The MiG-21 competed against the Su-7, a significantly larger and heavier fighter design, developed by Sukhoi Design Bureau (known at the time as OKB-51) in accordance with the general initiative of the Soviet government dating from October 1953 which called for the accelerated development of a generation of Mach 2-capable fighter types. Powered by the AL-7F engine, its swept-wing prototype, designated as the S-1, hit 2,170km/h; and in early 1958 the VVS command authorities saw it as a more capable design, sporting better performance than that of the MiG-21. The swept-wing S-1 and delta-wing T-3 prototypes developed by Sukhoi proved to be faster by 150–200km/h and demonstrated a higher practical ceiling by 1,000–1,500m (3,300–4,900ft) than their Mikoyan counterparts, the Ye-2 and Ye-4. Furthermore, the S-1's design maturity was judged to be better than that of the

The swept-wing Su-7 fighter was developed by the design bureau led by Pavel Sukhoi under a Soviet government initiative dating from September 1953, which called for the accelerated development of several Mach 2-capable fighter types. The Su-7 was a significantly larger and heavier jet than Mikoyan's Ye-2 and Ye-4. (Sukhoi Design Bureau via author)

The Ye-6/3 prototype seen armed with 16-round 57mm rocket packs and fitted with a 490-litre underfuselage drop tank. (Mikoyan & Gurevich Design Bureau via author)

OKB-155 aircraft; and this swept-wing prototype was also considered suitable for use in the fighter-bomber role thanks to its heavier warload.

In the event, the Soviet military and political leadership wisely decided that there was enough room and resources to allow follow-on development and serial production of both the lightweight Mikoyan and the heavyweight Sukhoi fighter designs. This way, the former evolved into a lightweight and affordable tactical (frontline) fighter with air-to-air and air-to-surface capabilities, while the latter was developed into the swept-wing Su-7 fighter-bomber for the VVS (optimized for delivery of tactical nuclear bombs) and the delta-wing Su-9 missile-armed fighter-interceptor for the Soviet Air Defence Forces (PVO).

MiG-21F launched in production

The series-production MiG-21F was designed following a Soviet government decree dated 24 July 1958 and the corresponding follow-on order issued by GKAT on 3 August 1958. The new lightweight fighter derivative of the Ye-5 was to be powered by an uprated R-11F-300 turbojet (which is why the letter 'F' in the designation was used to distinguish this specific version).

The improved engine, rated at 56.40kN (12,650lb st) with afterburner and 38.06kN (8,536lb st) at military power, retained the compressor, combustion chamber and turbine of its predecessor almost unchanged and added an improved afterburner section. The boosted afterburning rating promised a significant increase in performance, reflected in the performance requirements decreed of the MiG-21F, which needed to deliver 2,300–2,500km/h maximum level speed and 21,000–22,000m (68,900–72,200ft) practical ceiling. Ferry flight range requirements called for 1,400km range on internal fuel and up to 2,000km with an external tank, while flight endurance was to be no less than 1.5 and 2.25 hours respectively. Time for climbing to 20,000m (65,600ft) was required to be 8–10 minutes; take-off run length was to be up to 450m and the landing roll 450–850m.

The new version of the lightweight fighter, converted from existing MiG-21 airframes built at GAZ-31, was set for submission for its state testing effort with the NII-VVS in the fourth quarter of 1959. As many as 12 series-production examples were ordered for manufacture in Tbilisi, replacing on the assembly line the original MiG-21 version, already launched there. The decree also called for replacement of the two NR-30 cannon with one 30mm TKB-515, the addition of two heat-seeking air-to-air missiles (AAMs) and installation of the TsD-30 air-intercept radar set.

The first MiG-21F prototype, designated as the Ye-6/1, initially utilized the delta-wing design, inherited unchanged from the Ye-5 and featuring three aerodynamic fences. The second prototype, the Ye-6/2, introduced a modified wing design configuration, retaining only one fence, the change improving the aerodynamic performance and simplifying the manufacturing process. The pointed wingtips were also removed, the wing chord was increased at the rear and the aileron span was reduced. In the event, this successful wing design was retained almost unchanged on the follow-on MiG-21 versions built until the mid-1980s.

The Ye-6/1's tailplane was also enlarged and moved further to the rear, down to the mid-level and mounted horizontally, with the fixed roots eliminated. The rear fuselage was enlarged in both diameter and length to improve the aerodynamic performance, but the engine bay cooling inlets remained situated above the tailplanes. The third NR-30 cannon, to be installed on the rear, was finally deleted. Other modifications introduced into the Ye-6/2's design included a new circular air intake with sharp lips and a two-shock conical centre-body that slid axially in three positions: fully retraced at speeds up to Mach 1.5; intermediate for speeds from Mach 1.5 up to Mach 1.9; and fully forward for speeds exceeding Mach 1.9.

The Ye-6 also received a brake parachute, housed in a bay on the port underside of the rear fuselage, and introduced a dorsal fin which joined the dorsal spine and the fin, while the Ye-5's two ventral strakes were replaced by a single ventral fin on the Ye-6. The undernose pitot boom folded upwards on the ground to reduce the risk of damage caused by ground personnel and vehicles hitting it.

The avionics suite included the ASP-5N gyro lead-computing gunsight, intended to be offered together with an optional SIV-52 forward-looking infrared (FLIR) system for night visual intercepts, ARK-54I automated direction finder (ADF), MRP-56I marker beacon receiver and the KKO-3 oxygen equipment set.

The Ye-6/1 made its maiden flight on 20 May 1958, with Vladimir Nefyedov at the controls, and during initial tests it demonstrated very promising performance, reaching 2,181km/h, corresponding to Mach 2.05 at 12,050m (39,500ft). This prototype, however, had a very short life, as it was lost on its seventh flight on 28 May 1958, crashing onto the runway at Zhukovskii during an engine flame-out landing approach. The engine failed while the aircraft was flying at 18,000m (59,000ft) and the pilot attempted an emergency landing by gliding the unpowered fighter back to the airfield. Nefyedov lost both lateral and longitudinal control at the very end of the unpowered approach, just before touching down with the hydraulic system inoperative, while the back-up electrically driven pump (used to maintain pressure in the hydraulic system) proved ineffective. Following an ill-fated attempt at a flared landing, the Ye-6/1's undercarriage hit the runway hard, and it turned upside down and caught fire. The pilot was quickly recovered from the wreckage, but died from severe burns and other injures in the hospital later the same day.

The second and third MiG-21F prototypes, designated as the Ye-6/2 and Ye-6/3 respectively, continued the type's flight-test efforts and introduced a plethora of design refinements and improvements, such as a larger air intake cone, duplicated hydraulic system, additional fuel cells housed in the wings and the fuselage, auxiliary air inlets on both sides of the nose to prevent compressor stalls, an all-new SK ejection seat with blast protection for the pilot during bail-out, an increased-area fin and a larger ventral fin. The Ye-6/2, featuring a cleaner wing and two operative NR-30 cannon with 30 rounds each, took to the air for the first time on 15 September 1958, while the Ye-6/3 followed suit in December 1958. The latter was the first of the MiG-21 family to introduce yaw vanes on the pitot boom and the SRO-2 Khorm Identification Friend or Foe (IFF) transponder, as well as a 490-litre centreline drop tank.

The 61 factory test flights demonstrated that the MiG-21F's practical ceiling was 20,100m (65,920ft) whilst maintaining Mach 1.1 and the

The Ye-6/2 prototype received wingtip-mounted APU-13 rail launchers for the R-3S heat-seeking air-to-air missile, a fitment that necessitated wing modification, with the outer section's leading-edge sweep reduced to 48°. In the event this configuration proved to be too complicated. (Mikoyan & Gurevich Design Bureau via author)

The MiG-21F-13 was a basic daytime short-range interceptor and tactical fighter with a principal armament of two K-13 (R-3S) air-to-air missiles, carried on two underwing pylons, and one internal NR-30 cannon with 30 rounds only, or two 16-round rocket packs as seen here. (Author's collection)

maximum level speed in afterburner was Mach 2, equal to 2,100km/h at 15,000m (49,200ft). There were expectations that further design refinements would allow the maximum speed to be increased, initially to 2,300km/h and then to 2,500km/h. Time for climbing from sea level to the practical ceiling of 20,700m (67,900ft) in afterburner was 8 minutes 25 seconds, while at military power rating the practical ceiling was 14,500m (47,560ft).

In April 1959 the MiG-21F was submitted for state testing with the Soviet Air Force, and this was completed in November the same year. The final flight-test report, issued by the NII-VVS, noted that the MiG-21F had demonstrated good handling characteristics and stable engine operation; the aircraft was also judged as being simple to control, with its design features allowing operations from Class II airfields (i.e. capable to be operated from unpaved runways). In order to enhance the MiG-21F's overall combat capabilities in high-speed/high-altitude conditions, the report recommended integration of a new weapons suite consisting of two R-3S (K-13) air-to-air missiles and one NR-30 cannon; the report also recommended that this new missile-armed derivative should enter production as soon as possible.

Between 25 June 1960 and 20 April 1961 the MiG-21F underwent an extensive testing programme, undertaken by the NII-VVS, carrying an array of air-to-ground ordnance on the wing pylons (one under each wing), which had been equipped with BD3-58-21 adaptor beams. The weapons used in the ordnance trials included ARS-212M and S-24 large-calibre rockets as well as 100kg OFAB-100-120, 250kg FAB-250-270 and FAB-250M-54 and 500kg FAB-500M-54 free-fall bombs, and ZAB-360 napalm canisters. S-5 57mm rockets, fired from 16-round UB-16-57UM packs, useful against both air and ground targets, had undergone testing and evaluation on the MiG-21 at an earlier stage in 1960.

Serial production of the MiG-21F was launched at GAZ-21 in Gorkii in 1959. The first example took to the air on 8 February 1960 and the production run in 1960 and 1961 accounted for 79 examples. After that the MiG-21F was replaced by the follow-on Fishbed derivative, boasting guided missile armament and a plethora of small airframe improvements. In addition, GAZ-31 added ten more MiG-21Fs, all of which were rolled out in 1959. Three of these were eventually handed over to OKB-155 for conversion into the MiG-21F-13 version, while the other seven examples were delivered to both the design bureau and the Flight Test Institute at Zhukovskii for use as experimental aircraft in various development programmes, as well as in a series of reliability trials.

Ye-6T testbed

Upon completion of the MiG-21F's state flight testing with the NII-VVS, the second and third Ye-6 prototypes were modified as testbeds for use in follow-on flight testing and evaluation

programmes undertaken by OKB-155. The first of these machines, redesignated as the Ye-6T/1, powered by an increased-thrust R-11F2-300 turbojet with afterburning rating of 60.82kN (13,640lb st) and featuring an enlarged intake centrebody cone, was intended for dynamic ceiling trials. Flown by Georgii Mosolov under the false designation Ye-66, it established a world speed record of 2,388km/h on 31 October 1958. In 1959, the same pilot, flying the same experimental aircraft, broke that record when he flew the Ye-6T/1 at 2,504km/h in level flight, corresponding to Mach 2.38. In 1960

another OKB-155 pilot, Konstatin Kokkinaki, established another world speed record with the Ye-66 while flying a closed-loop route of 100km, reaching 2,146.66km/h. On 28 April 1961 Mosolov again managed to break a world record with the Ye-66A, this time climbing to 34,714m (113,862ft) using a mixed powerplant comprised of the R-11F2-300 turbojet and the S3-20M5A liquid-fuel rocket motor, rated at 29.43kN (6,600lb st) at sea level and working for 100 seconds.

The R-3S (AA-2 *Atoll*), a copy of the American AIM-9B Sidewinder short-range AAM, was the first Soviet mass-produced heat-seeking missile, and was used by the MiG-21F-13 as its principal armament in the interceptor role. (Author's collection)

The second experimental prototype, known as the Ye-6T/3, was used to test the uprated R-11F-300 engine with adjustable afterburner, and had its internal fuel capacity increased by some 140 litres. It was also equipped with the KAP-1 autopilot, working in the roll axis, and modified to test foreplanes (also known as destabilizing pivoted canards) in order to support the Ye-8 development programme, as well as receiving the new RSIU-5V communications radio. The purpose of the foreplanes was to enhance supersonic manoeuvrability, as these newly added surfaces reduced the aircraft's inherent longitudinal stability at supersonic speeds. The Ye-6T/3, fitted with APU-13 rail launchers on modified wingtips, was also used as a test platform for the launch equipment used by the R-3S guided AAM.

MiG-21F-13 guided missile interceptor

The Ye-6/T1, Ye-6T/2 and Ye-6/3 prototypes were used to support the MiG-21F-13 (OKB-155 internal designation Type 74) development and flight-test programme, undertaken in the second half of 1958 using three MiG-21Fs built at GAZ-31 and converted to the F-13 configuration, followed by seven more in 1959.

The MiG-21F-13 was a basic lightweight, daytime, short-range, clear-weather interceptor and tactical fighter. Its principal armament of two R-3S heat-seeking air-to-air missiles was carried on two APU-28 rail launchers, later replaced by the APU-13, attached to BD3-58-21 adaptor beams, one under each wing. The MiG-21F-13 also retained one internal NR-30 30mm cannon on the starboard side, with only 30 rounds. The alternative ordnance in the fighter-interceptor role consisted of two UB-16-57UM rocket packs, each loaded with 16 S-5M 57mm rockets, instead of the R-3S missiles. These rockets were judged as an effective weapon, particularly when fired from close range against large bombers and transport aircraft, but they were ill-suited for use against manoeuvring fighters.

The MiG-21F-13's canopy of blown acrylic with a bulletproof windscreen hinged at the front provided good visibility for the pilot in all directions – something that was not provided in the follow-on derivatives of the Fishbed. (Author's collection)

For ground attacks the MiG-21F-13 was cleared to carry two UB-16-57UM rocket packs, each containing 16 S-5 57mm rockets, or two ARS-212 or ARS-240 (S-24) missiles or 250/500kg high-drag, high-explosive bombs.

The MiG-21F-13 was also equipped with the SIV-52 FLIR sensor for night-time intercepts, integrated with the ASP-5ND gunsight. It was a rather primitive night-vision system for clear-weather intercepts, limited for use at altitudes up to 9,000m (29,500ft) and with a maximum detection range against a twin-engine bomber of 4km.

The MiG-21F-13 was designed from the outset to intercept transonic/supersonic bombers and fighter-bombers at altitudes up to 20,000m (65,600ft). Interceptions were limited to rear-hemisphere attacks only, using the rudimentary SRD-5M Kvant radar rangefinder with a range of 0.5–7km. The Kvant provided missile launch and gun-firing distances; the associated ASP-5ND gunsight was used to assist accurate aiming during gun- and rocket-firing runs on both air and ground targets. In real-world conditions, MiG-21F-13 intercepts were critically dependent on guidance from a ground control station – manned by a dedicated Ground Control Intercept (GCI) officer using voice commands to transfer speed, altitude and heading commands – until the target was visually acquired.

Frontline pilots tended to comment that among the chief shortcomings of the MiG-21F-13 were its very high landing speed (exceeding 270km/h) and the rather crude cockpit arrangement, the latter an ergonomic nightmare similar to those of the MiG-19S and MiG-17F. On the other hand, the MiG-21F-13 proved to be the most agile variant of the entire Fishbed family and the cockpit glazing afforded pretty good all-round visibility – a useful advantage for air combat manoeuvring.

The first MiG-21F-13s for the frontline units of the Soviet Air Force's Frontal Aviation (FA-VVS) arm were taken on strength in 1961. During series production, a plethora of improvements were adopted; these included additional internal fuel tanks in the fuselage and the wings as well as an increased-chord fin with an area of $4.73m^2$ compared to $3.80m^2$ on the initial production MiG-21F-13. Total internal fuel capacity reached 2,550 litres; in addition, the centreline pylon was modified to carry one 490-litre drop tank. The MiG-21F-13 also received a limited reconnaissance capability thanks to the provision for installing an AFA-39 camera in a bay aft of the nose wheel.

In December 1959 a decree for discontinuing MiG-21F production at GAZ-21 was issued by GKAT as it was to be quickly superseded by the improved MiG-21F-13 Fishbed-C. As many as 532 MiG-21F-13s for the Soviet Air Force rolled off the line at GAZ-21 in Gorkii (in 1960, 132 aircraft were rolled out; in 1961 the number was

FISHBED PRODUCTION BY PLANTS

GAZ-21 (Gorkii, now known as Nizhnii Novgorod, Russia) – 5,532 MiG-21s built between 1958 and 1985, of which 1,812 were destined for export customers.

GAZ-30 (Moscow, Russia) – 3,203 MiG-21s built between 1962 and 1977, almost all of them destined for export customers; this number included no fewer than 230 MiG-21U examples built between 1964 and 1968.

GAZ-31 (Tbilisi, Georgia) – 1,660 MiG-21U/US/UM two-seaters built between 1962 and 1985; 10 MiG-21Fs in 1959.

Aero Vodochody (Prague, Czechoslovakia) – 194 MiG-21F-13s built between 1961 and 1972.

HAL Nasik (Nasik, India) – 54 MiG-21FLs assembled from component knocked-down kits (manufactured at GAZ-21) supplied by the Soviet Union; 205 locally produced examples of the type between 1967 and 1973. The MiG-21M/MF (Type 88) was in production at HAL between 1973 and 1981, with 158 built. Sixty-five MiG-21bis were assembled from component knocked-down kits (manufactured at GAZ-21) and 220 more MiG-21bis were locally produced examples.

Shenyang Aviation Plant (Shenyang, China) – 13 MiG-21F-13s assembled from component knocked-down kits (manufactured at GAZ-21) supplied by the Soviet Union in 1961–62. Follow-on production of th J-7/JJ7 family was non-licensed.

232 and the first ten months of 1962 saw production of 168 more), but this model remained in production for less than three years before being replaced in 1962 by the MiG-21PF radar-equipped interceptor. MiG-21F-13 production for export customers began in 1962 at GAZ-30 in Moscow; later, its licence production was handed over to the Aero Vodochody company in Czechoslovakia, where the type received the local designation S-106. In early 1961 the MiG-21F-13 production licence was also provided to the People's Republic of China (PRC), with two pattern aircraft and a number of component knocked-down kits delivered there. In the event, the Chinese licence-production programme proved to be a failure due to China's abrupt split with the Soviet Union. As a result of the split, the Chinese aircraft industry experienced huge difficulties and delays in its drive to establish a working non-license production line for the fighter which received the local designation J-7.

TECHNICAL SPECIFICATIONS (MiG-21PFM, TYPE 94)

Fuselage

The MiG-21 featured an all-metal semi-monocoque fuselage of almost circular cross-section. The main construction materials used in the airframe and wing structure comprised of aluminium alloys, mainly the D16-T, V65-1 and V-25 types, as well as high-strength steel alloys such as the 30KhGSA and 30KhGSHN2A types.

Maximum fuselage width was 1,242mm and it was manufactured in two principal sections, joined just behind the fixed part of the wing, at frames 28 and 28A. The forward section included the circular ram-air intake 870mm in diameter, with a three-position movable conical centrebody driven forward and aft automatically by a hydraulic actuator; its position depended on the current speed, angle of attack and tailplane deflection. The centrebody was fully retracted up to Mach 1.5, had an intermediate position from Mach 1.5 to Mach 1.9 depending on the speed, and extended to a full forward position above Mach 1.9 in order to focus shock waves on the inlet lip and reduce the air intake area. The centrebody's travel from full forward to full aft position was 200mm; it was also possible for it to be pulled forward a further 800mm for servicing of the radar. Cooling was provided by using bleed air entering via a ring surrounding the base of the cone; boundary layer air was sucked in by aft-facing ejectors above and below the nose. At speeds exceeding March 1.35 the airflow was stopped as the air was heated to a degree unusable for cooling purposes; flight duration at such speeds was short enough and no overheating was expected to occur in high-altitude flight.

The top of the nose contained the PVD-5 pitot boom, mounted at the top of the nose inlet, and a large forward-hinged door for access to the avionics boxes housed in a bay stretching from frames 3 to 6. The nose undercarriage leg was attached to frame 6, together with an armoured plate. The cockpit section was located between frames 6 and 11, with the battery bay situated under the floor.

Rectangular automatic inlet doors on each side of the nose opened inwards to improve airflow into the air duct in yawed flight and to avoid compressor stalls. Around the cockpit, beginning at frame 6, the air duct split into two and at frame 22 the ducts came together with a circular cross-section just before the engine compressor. Automatic inlets were installed next to frame 10 on each side, provided with spring-loaded suck-in doors to supply additional air in conditions of high power demand and insufficient ram air pressure. The dorsal fuel tanks were housed in the fuselage behind the cockpit, between frames 11 and 28. The bulged dorsal fairing along the top of the fuselage housed control pushrods, avionics, a single-point refuelling cap and a fuel tank, the last of which was installed behind frame 11. The forward-hinged petal-type airbrakes, deflecting at 20°, were attached each side of the underfuselage, hinging on frame 11 and below the wing leading edge, while the third brake unit, deflecting at 40°, was attached onto the underfuselage, forward of the ventral fin. Above and below the wing, on each side, blister fairings were added to accommodate the main wheels when retracted. The main undercarriage units retracted into a bay located between frames 16 and 20.

The tail section of the fuselage, secured by 18 bolts, comprised of 13 frames and was detachable from frame 28A. The engine bay extended from frames 29 to 34, with a vertical fin extending over almost the entire length of this section with 352mm maximum depth. The vertical fin had 60° leading-edge sweepback and used a symmetric S-11 aerofoil profile. Thickness/chord ratio was 6 per cent and surface area was 5.32m².

Wings and undercarriage

The MiG-21 was a cantilever mid-wing monoplane of clipped delta planform using the TsAGI S-12 symmetrical aerofoil profile: thickness/chord ratio was 5 per cent at root and 4.2 per cent at tip; span was 7.154m and area 23m². Leading-edge sweepback was 57° with 2° anhedral from roots and zero incidence; there was no leading-edge camber. The structure consisted of one main spar, one chief transverse spar, secondary spars at the leading and trailing edge of the fixed part of the wing, 26 ribs ahead of the main spar, perpendicular to the leading edge and 12 ribs behind the chief transverse spar, parallel to the longitudinal axis.

The wings were attached to the fuselage by forged and machined root ribs with eight attachment points on five fuselage frames. A small aerodynamic fence was installed on the upper surface of each wing 670mm from the tip.

The large rectangular 'blown' hinged flaps were hydraulically extended to a maximum of 24.5° for take-off and 44.5° for landing, while in-flight deflection was limited to 20°. The 'blown' flaps used hot and high-pressure air, bled from the engine compressor and blown across the flap in an effort to increase lift and reduce landing speed by some 40km/h. Flap area was 0.935m² each.

The landing gear was hydraulically retractable, of tricycle type, with a single wheel on each unit. Track was 2,692mm and wheelbase 4,806mm. All units were housed in the fuselage when retracted. The main landing gears pivoted inwards at 87° at the junction of the main and transverse wing spars and folded into the triangular space between them. The main wheels turned to stow vertically inside the fuselage, outboard of the air duct between fuselage frames 16 and 20; doors were hinged from below by their own hydraulic jack. The main wheels were of KT-92B type and had tyre size 800 × 200mm, inflated to between 7.8 and 10.1 bars (113 and 146.45lb/sq in).

The forward-retracting non-steerable nose wheel unit, housed in a narrow bay between frames 3 and 6, used a KT-102 wheel with tyre size 500 × 180mm (normal inflation pressure 5.8 bars [85.1lb/sq in]), with a free-swivelling wheel deflected at 47° left and right during taxying.

All wheels were provided with pneumatic disk brakes, supplied from compressed-air bottles. Steering was provided by differential main wheel braking. All undercarriage units were provided with hydraulic and mechanical downlocks and mechanical uplocks, with emergency compressed-air bottles for extension. The PT-6282 cruciform brake parachute had a 19m² area and was housed inside a fairing at the base of the rudder.

Flight controls

The conventional hydraulically boosted tapered tabless ailerons were incorporated inset for lateral control (in the roll axis); each deflected 20° up and down, driven by the BU-45 irreversible booster units. Longitudinal control (in the pitch axis) was provided by horizontal all-moving hydraulically boosted tailplanes with no anhedral, carried on swept hinge spigots. Tailplane profile was A6A symmetric, with a thickness/chord ratio of 6 per cent, a leading edge sweep of 55° and a total area of 3.94m², while span (including tip and anti-flutter masses) was 3.74m. The tailplanes deflected from +7° to -16.5°, driven by two chambers (one in each hydraulic system), and featured two gearing ratios for use in accordance with speed and altitude, adjusted by the ARU-3V system. The tailplane lacked trim tabs and its electrical rocking trim switch was situated on the control column. The hydraulically boosted rudder, providing control in the lateral axis (in yaw), was provided with aerodynamic and mass balance and was carried on three hinges, deflected at 25° left and right. The KAP-2 single-channel autopilot provided improved control and stabilization in the roll axis only.

Airframe systems

The electrical system in the aircraft was single-phase 115V/400Hz and three-phase 365V/400Hz AC. Electricity was supplied by a GSR-ST-1200VT-2I engine-driven DC generator, which was also used as a starter, drawing power from two silver/zinc batteries. There were two transformers (to supply 115V/400Hz and three-phase 365V/400Hz AC) serving all the avionics and instrumentation, lighting, armament control and windscreen de-icing equipment.

The aircraft featured dual independent engine-driven hydraulic systems (general and booster), each supplied by an engine-driven pump. The general system operated the nose cone, auxiliary inlet doors, undercarriage, airbrakes, flaps, afterburner nozzle, automatic brakes (to stop wheel rotation at take-off), one chamber of the tailplane power unit and the back-up aileron drive. The booster system served the normal aileron operation and the other half of the tailplane power unit. Both systems ran at a pressure of 180–215 bars (2,610–3,118lb/sq in).

The two pneumatic systems – general and emergency – were charged by an engine-driven air compressor. The general system served the wheel brakes, canopy seal, canopy anti-ice/demist, VKK-4 or VKK-6 pilot anti-G suit and braking parachute deployment, while the emergency system served the undercarriage extension and wheel brakes. All air bottles were capable of recharging in the air or from a ground-based pressurized-air supply unit. Air was also supplied to the pilot's

The MiG-21PFM was the classic representative of the first-generation interceptors of the Fishbed family – fast and light, armed with two AAMs only and capable of carrying air-to-ground ordnance of up to 1,000kg. (Author's collection)

The MiG-21PFM's cockpit, dominated by the large radar scope located in the central area of the instrument panel. The artificial horizon is situated below it. (Author)

VK-3 ventilation suit, worn in low-to-medium level operations in hot-climate conditions.

The gaseous oxygen was stored in six bottles, housed in the wing root, and was supplied by the KKO-5 oxygen gauge to the pilot's pressurized flight suit and the GSh-6 enclosed pressure helmet, being operated manually or automatically at high altitude and in the event of emergency loss of cockpit pressure. In normal operation, up to 2,000m (6,600ft), the KP-2 gauge supplied the KM-3 pilot oxygen mask (used in conjunction with the ZSh-3 helmet) or the GSh-6 pressure helmet with pure air only; above that altitude it provided an air-oxygen mixture with a varying proportion of oxygen; above 8,000m (26,200ft), only pure oxygen was supplied.

Cockpit

The instrument panel was painted in black and dominated by a large radar scope, provided with a deep sun hood. The PKI-1 collimator gunsight was installed on top of the windscreen frame; it was used for visually aiming the RS-2US and R-3S missiles as well as the S-5 rockets on air and ground targets in shallow/steep dive or horizontal flight, and also for aiming the GSh-23 gun (housed in the GP-9 conformal gun-pod).

The canopy featured a fixed, flat and bulletproof windscreen and a movable main section hinged to starboard. The windscreen was equipped with an alcohol de-icing system. The KM-1M ejection seat was cleared for use at ground level in level flight at a minimum speed of 130km/h, while the maximum indicated speed for safe escape was 1,100km/h at all altitudes. The ejection sequence was initiated by the pilot by pulling up the twin ejection handles located on the seat between his legs. The canopy was jettisoned before booster firing was initiated by using pyrotechnical cartridges. In addition, there was a back-up canopy jettison function provided to the pilot in case of failure of the primary jettison mechanism, activated by pulling a dedicated handle (the seat ejection sequence cannot be initiated without canopy jettison).

The KM-1M provided safe ejection up to 25,000m (82,000ft). In the event of an ejection initiated at ground level, the seat was ejected to 45m (148ft) altitude, using a solid-fuel booster, resulting in a force of 20G acceleration acting on the pilot for 0.38 seconds. The seat contained an SPS-M pilot rescue parachute, a NAZ-U survival kit with an MLAS-1 life raft, as well as the KP-27M and KP-52M oxygen gauges used to supply oxygen to the pilot in the event of a high-altitude ejection.

Engine

The R-11F2S-300 turbojet was rated at 60.58kN (13,613lb st) at full afterburner and 38.25kN (8,598lb st) dry (military power), with flap blowing inoperative, while its weight was 1,165kg.

Accommodated inside the fuselage, beginning at frame 22 to the rear end, the engine was provided with two attachment points to the fuselage, at frame 25 (forward) and 28 (rear). The powerplant featured auxiliary systems for cooling the engine bay, inlet and engine control, fuel supply, fire-extinguishing and oxygen supply for in-flight relight.

A twin-spool turbojet, the R-11F2S-300 featured a simple low-pressure compressor with only three axial stages, driven by a single-stage low-pressure turbine with solid shrouded blades. The high-pressure compressor featured three stages and was driven by the high-pressure turbine. The can-annular combustor featured ten combustion chambers, each provided with twin igniters, and the axial turbine had two stages. The afterburner was provided with three spray rings and a multi-flap variable cross-section nozzle, controlled by an electrically signalled hydraulic system with three rams driving an actuation ring. The engine sported a pilot-selectable second stage of afterburner used to reduce acceleration time to supersonic speed.

The R-13-300 engine was a follow-on development of the original R-11F2-300, utilizing the same basic design and developing some 63.70kN (13,400lb st) at maximum afterburner and 39.90kN (8,973lb st) at military power (dry) rating. (Author)

Engine control from 'Stop' to 'Full Afterburner' power setting positions of the throttle was provided by the PURT-1F system, working together with the NR-21F2 primary fuel pump/precise electro-mechanical regulator unit; it was used to maintain constant rpm under normal flight conditions, thrust being varied by fuel flow changes. Another NR-21F2 pump/electro-mechanical regulator unit managed the afterburner operation.

An auxiliary gearbox on the bottom of the engine housed a GSR-12000VRT DC starter/generator, an SGO-8 AC generator, two NP34M-1T hydraulic pumps, a DTsN-13-D1 fuel pump and a DTE-1 rpm sensor. Bleed air, taken from the sixth stage, was supplied to the cockpit environment control system, fuel and hydraulic tanks.

Two SPRD-99 rocket boosters, each rated at 24.52kN (5,512lb st) for up to 17 seconds, fitted under the rear fuselage, aft of the main wheel doors, were used for shortening the take-off run.

Fuel system

The MiG-21PFM's fuel system incorporated six cells in the fuselage, two forward and two rear integral wing tanks and a dorsal tank pack with a total capacity of 2,680 litres, of which the usable internal fuel was 2,480 litres, representing a total load of 1,984kg. The internal tankage was augmented by one centreline finned aluminium drop tank with a capacity of 490 litres, usable to Mach 1.6; there was also provision for use of an 800-litre centreline tank. The fuel used was of T-1, TS-1 or T-2 type and the minimum fuel capacity for take-off was set at 1,400 litres. All tanks were provided with a pressurization system using bleed air supplied from the last compressor stage. The tanks were filled through an open and centralized gravity filler cap located on the dorsal tank 7.

Navigation, communication and IFF equipment

The navigation components of the avionics suite included the KSI-1 heading reference system, the ARK-10 ADF, the MRP-56P marker beacon receiver and the RV-UM low-altitude radar altimeter. The aircraft was equipped with a single R-802V (RSIU-5V) VHF/UHF communication radio. The IFF system

The RS-2US, carried on the inner pylon, was a beam-riding AAM for use against non-manoeuvring bombers and proved entirely unsuitable in dogfights, while the R-3R, seen on the outer pylon, was a considerably more modern weapon utilizing the radar semi-active homing method. This, however, is not a representative configuration, as usually the MiG-21s carried one radar-guided and one heat-seeking missile under each wing. (Author)

incorporated the SRZO-2M Khorm-Nikel interrogator/transponder and the SRO-2 transponder. The aircraft was also equipped with the SOD-57M air traffic control decimetric transponder.

Ordnance

GP-9 gun-pod
The MiG-21PFM was armed with one GSh-23L twin-barrel cannon housed in a conformal GP-9 gun-pod and provided with 200 rounds. It was developed in 1968, upon request from the Indian Air Force for arming the MiG-21FL, originally supplied as a missile-only armed interceptor, derived from the MiG-21PF. The pod was carried on the centreline pylon by using three attachment points, but the attachment itself was not rigid enough and this caused unwanted vibrations with subsequent dispersion of the fired shells, thus adversely affecting the gun's accuracy at longer ranges. As a rule, each GP-9 pod was individually fitted and aligned to a specific aircraft, which precluded any usable degree of interchangeability. When armed with the GP-9 pod, the short-legged MiG-21PFM/FL lacked the capability to carry a centreline drop tank, which further reduced range and endurance.

The GSh-23L was a rapid-fire lightweight and compact cannon, developed in the early 1960s, which unlike on previous MiGs could be fired without gases affecting the engine. It was made capable of unleashing 174–196-gram rounds at a muzzle velocity of 680–730m/s and at a rate of fire of 3,200rpm, effective at distances up to 800m. The cannon was aimed by the MiG-21PFM pilot using the World War II-vintage PKI-1 simple collimator gunsight with fixed graticule, optimized for use against non-manoeuvring targets, without any gyro compensation and lead computation capability; the lead was generated manually according to the visual estimation of the pilot who used the fixed graticule with mils marks.

Air-to-air missiles
The R-3S (K-13) AAM was a reverse-engineered copy of the American AIM-9B Sidewinder heat-seeking AAM, with an effective range at low altitude of 0.5–2km, which at high altitude extended to 9km. In the 1970s a proportion of the MiG-21PFMs serving with the Soviet Air Force and Warsaw Pact fighter regiments were modified for use of the vastly improved R-3M (K-13M) missile.

The RS-2US (K-5) was a 1950s-vintage guided weapon designed originally for use with the RP-5 air-intercept radar of the MiG-19PM, and was effective only against non-manoeuvring targets. Originally built for use against bombers, its warhead weighted 13kg. The missile proved very sensitive to the

 FULL MiG-21BIS ARMAMENT BREAKDOWN
1. R-60 air-to-air missile
2. R-3S air-to-air missile
3. R-13M air-to-air missile
4. R-3R air-to-air missile
5. R-55 air-to-air missile
6. RS-2US air-to-air missile
7. Kh-66 air-to-surface missile
8. S-24 240mm rocket
9. UB-16-57UM rocket pack
10. S-5 57mm rocket
11. OFAB-100-120 free-fall bomb
12. OFAB-250-270 free-fall bomb
13. FAB-500M54 free-fall bomb
14. ZAB-360 napalm canister
15. GSh-23L twin-barrel cannon

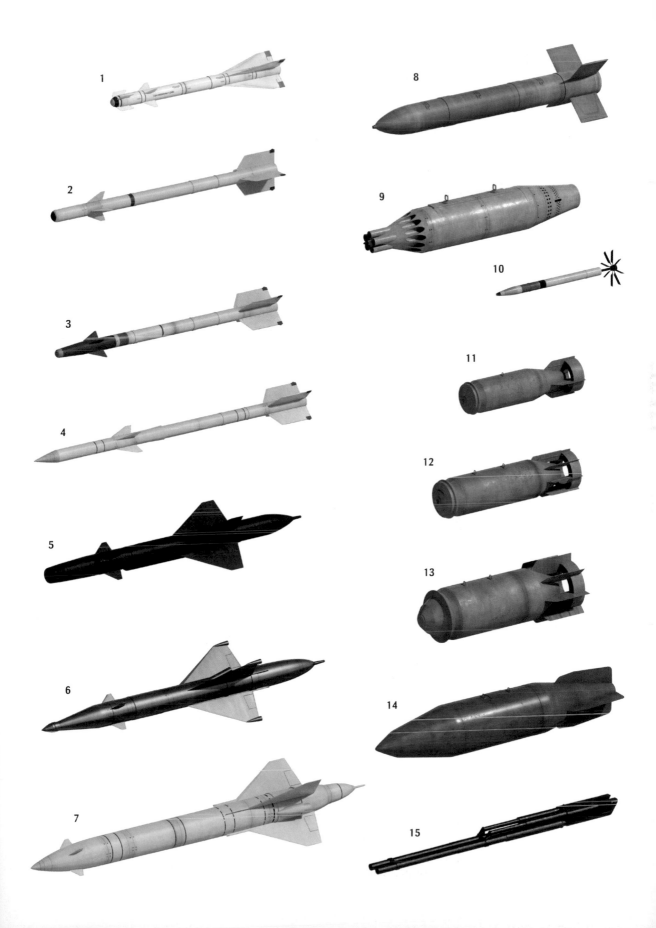

THE MiG-21PFM'S IN-FLIGHT LIMITATIONS

The Fishbed-F was limited to a Mach 2.05 maximum speed at high altitude when 'clean' or armed with two air-to-air missiles. When carrying a centreline fuel tank the maximum Mach number was reduced to 1.6. At speeds exceeding these figures the directional stability decreased to a level deemed insufficient to guarantee safe and stable flight. When carrying bombs the fighter was cleared for Mach 1.3; with the GP-9 gun-pod a limitation of Mach 1.8 was imposed. Both of these Mach limits were imposed due to the strength limitations of the external stores.

With regard to the maximum permissible indicated speed when 'clean' or armed with two R-3S AAMs, the MiG-21PFM was limited to 1,100km/h when flying at altitudes below 2,000m (6,600ft) and to 1,200km/h above 2,200m (7,220ft). When carrying two RS-2US AAMs the maximum indicated speed was limited to 1,200km/h above 5,000m (16,400ft). This type of speed limit was imposed due to airframe structural (i.e. skin, hatches, canopy, etc.) and external stores strength considerations.

The destructive load for the MiG-21 airframe structure was set at 11–12G. The G-load limitation when 'clean' or armed with two R-3S missiles at speeds below Mach 0.8 was not to exceed 7G with more than 2,000 litres of remaining fuel, while with less than 1,600 litres in the tanks the limitation was 8.5G. At speeds above Mach 0.8 the structural load limitation with more than 1,600 litres of fuel was 6G, while with less than 1,600 litres it increased to 7G. When carrying the GP-9 gun-pod or bombs the MiG-21PFM was stressed up to 6G; equipped with a 490-litre centreline tank, up to 5G; and with an 800-litre centreline tank, up to 4G.

The R-11F2S-300 engine was limited to 10 minutes of operation in idle mode and 1 minute in military power mode on the ground; maximum permissible time in maximum afterburner on the ground was set at 15 seconds. The engine was cleared for operation at altitudes up to 15,000m (49,200ft) with the following limitations: the afterburner was allowed to be engaged at speeds above 600km/h after take-off and 500km/h in flight. Reducing the rating below military power was allowed at speeds up to 1,100km/h at altitudes below 2,000m (6,600ft) and at speeds up to 1,200km/h at 2,000–8,000m (6,600–26,200ft).

radar beam shape of the launch platform and its movements, and was also prone to jamming. The effective range at low altitude was 2.5–5km, while at high altitude it extended to 6.5km.

Air-to-ground missiles

The Kh-66 was an air-to-ground guided missile which was cleared for use by the MiG-21PFM in 1968. Weighing 278kg, it was equipped with a 103kg warhead and the launch range was 3–10km. The Kh-66 was a beam-riding missile and the MiG-21PFM used the RP-21M radar in the fixed forward mode to provide guidance, with the beam put on the target while in the aircraft was in a shallow dive; the pilot was required to aim the Kh-66 visually by using the PKI-1 collimator gunsight. The missile was rarely used in training flights; instead, for training purposes surplus RS-2US AAMs (featuring the same guidance method) were employed by the Soviet Air Force's fighter and fighter-bomber regiments, fired against ground targets (it proved to be precise enough in this role).

Unguided ordnance

The unguided weapons selection included two UB-16-57 16-round or two UB-32M 32-round rocket packs for firing the S-5 series of 57mm folding-fin rockets, or two S-24 240mm rockets on APU-7 launcher rails. The bomb load included up to eight OFAB-100-120 high-drag 100kg bombs on two MBD2-67 four-position racks. Two 250kg FAB-250M-54/M-58 free-fall bombs or two 500kg FAB-500M-54 free-fall bombs were carried on BD3-60-21D adaptor beams; and the MiG-21PFM was also capable of carrying two ZAB-360 napalm canisters, attached by D3-57 latches.

RP-21M radar

The RP-21M radar equipping the Soviet and Warsaw Pact MiG-21PFMs used a single parabolic conical-scan antenna housed in the nose centrebody. It featured a 15km detection range against a fighter-size target and the tracking range was 10km, while against bombers these ranges increased up to 20km and 15km respectively. The radar's single parabolic antenna was 550mm in diameter; it mechanically scanned in bars 30° left/right (in azimuth) and 6° up/down (in elevation), while tracking was performed in a narrower range – 5° left/right and up/down. The RP-21M operated in four different modes: search, acquisition, pursuit tracking and fire control.

The RP-21M was a rather primitive air-intercept radar system, lacking any look-down/shoot-down capability, and the minimum target altitude during low-level intercepts was restricted to 1,000m (3,300ft), while the low-level tracking range below 2,000m (6,600ft) did not exceed 5km. Below this altitude, intercepts had to be carried out visually; but even the R-3S missile is said to have often failed to achieve a stable lock-on due to the seeker head picking up a lot of ground clutter, especially while flying over hot terrain.

Self-protection systems

The MiG-21PFM used the SPS-141 response jammer to provide self-escort protection against a range of air and ground radar threats, working in pulse, quasi-continuous and continuous modes. The jammer was optimized to operate against missile- and artillery-guidance radars tracking the aircraft by disrupting both the angular tracking and rangefinding channels. There was also an option of employing two SPS-141-equipped aircraft as escort jammer platforms, using the so-called 'blinking' jamming method, causing the tracking radar to switch between the two aircraft all the time without getting a stable lock-on. The ASO-2I-E7R dispenser was another self-protection system housed in the same pod; it contained 64 IPP-26 infrared flares, ejected in a total of 16 series in the automatic mode of operation, each series containing four heat-emitting flares. When used to decoy surface-launched heat-seeking missiles in low-altitude flight, the interval between flares in each of the series was set at one second; when decoying air-to-air heat-seeking missiles the interval was 0.3 seconds.

MiG-21 dimensions

MiG-21 variant	Wingspan	Length (excluding pitot boom)	Height	Wing area, gross
MiG-21F-13	7.154m (23ft 5⅝in)	13.46m (44ft 1⅞in)	4.10m (13ft 5in)	23.0m² (247.6sq ft)
MiG-21PFM	7.154m (23ft 5⅝in)	14.10m (46ft 3⅓in)	4.125m (13ft 6in)	23.0m² (247.6sq ft)
MiG-21SM	7.154m (23ft 5⅝in)	14.185m (46ft 6½in)	4.125m (13ft 6in)	23.0m² (247.6sq ft)
MiG-21SMT	7.154m (23ft 5⅝in)	14.10m (46ft 3⅓in)	4.125m (13ft 6in)	23.0m² (247.6sq ft)
MiG-21bis	7.154m (23ft 5⅝in)	14.10m (46ft 3⅓in)	4.125m (13ft 6in)	23.0m² (247.6sq ft)
MiG-21UM	7.154m (23ft 5⅝in)	13.46m (44ft 1⅞in)	4.10m (13ft 5in)	23.0m² (247.6sq ft)

MiG-21 weights

MiG-21 variant	Empty	Normal	Max. take-off	Max. warload
MiG-21F-13	4,819kg (10,602lb)	7,100kg (15,620lb)	8,376kg (18,427lb)	1,000kg (2,200lb)
MiG-21PFM	5,383kg (11,843lb)	7,750kg (17,050lb)	8,238kg (18,124lb)	1,000kg (2,200lb)
MiG-21SM	5,998kg (13,196lb)	8,330kg (18,326lb)	9,400kg (20,680lb)	2,000kg (4,400lb)
MiG-21MF	5,350kg (11,770lb)	8,150kg (17,930lb)	9,400kg (20,680lb)	2,000kg (4,400lb)
MiG-21SMT	5,700kg (12,540lb)	8,400kg (18,480lb)	10,100kg (22,220lb)	2,000kg (4,400lb)
MiG-21bis	5,450kg (11,990lb)	8,725kg (19,195lb)	10,400kg (22,880lb)	2,000kg (4,400lb)
MiG-21UM	5,380kg (11,836lb)	8,000kg (17,600lb)	8,376kg (18,427lb)	1,000kg (2,200lb)

MiG-21 performance					
MiG-21 variant	Max. speed sea level	Max. speed high level	Service ceiling	Range	Rate of climb
MiG-21F-13	1,200km/h (745.65mph)	2,175km/h (1,351.48mph)	19,000m (62,300ft)	1,420km (882.35 miles)	138m/sec (27,158ft/min)
MiG-21PFM	1,200km/h (745.65mph)	2,175km/h (1,351.48mph)	19,000m (62,300ft)	1,670km (1,037.69 miles)	125m/sec (24,600ft/min)
MiG-21SM	1,200km/h (745.65mph)	2,230km/h (1,385.66mph)	18,000m (59,000ft)	1,240km (770.50 miles)	120m/sec (23,616ft/min)
MiG-21SMT	1,200km/h (745.65mph)	2,175km/h (1,351.48mph)	17,000m (55,800ft)	1,300km (807.78 miles)	120m/sec (23,616ft/min)
MiG-21bis	1,200km/h (745.65mph)	2,175km/h (1,351.48mph)	17,500m (57,400ft)	1,225km (761.18 miles)	235m/sec (46,248ft/min)
MiG-21UM	1,200km/h (745.65mph)	2,175km/h (1,351.48mph)	17,700m (58,000ft)	1,210km (751.86 miles)	130m/sec (25,584ft/min)

MiG-21 variant	Time to climb to height	Take-off run	Landing roll	Design load factor
MiG-21F-13	19,000m (62,300ft) in 13.5 min	900m (2,952ft)	900m (2,952ft)	7G
MiG-21PFM	18,000m (59,000ft) in 8 min	900m (2,952ft)	750m (2,461ft)	8.5G
MiG-21SM	17,500m (57,400ft) in 9 min	900m (2,952ft)	550m (1,804ft)	8.5G
MiG-21SMT	16,800m (55,100ft) in 9 min	950m (3,116ft)	550m (1,804ft)	8.5G
MiG-21bis	17,000m (55,800ft) in 8.5 min	830m (2,722ft)	550m (1,804ft)	8.5G
MiG-21UM	16,800m (55,100ft) in 8 min	900m (2,952ft)	550m (1,804ft)	7G

Main production (1958–85)			
MiG-21 variant	Number built	First flight	Production Period/Factory
MiG-21F	10 83	1958	1958/GAZ-31 1959–60/GAZ-21
MiG-21F-13	539 513 194	1959	1960–62/GAZ-21 1962–64/GAZ-30 1961–72/Aero Vodochody
MiG-21PF/PFS	525 n/a	1960	1961–65/GAZ-21 1964–66/GAZ-30
MiG-21PFM	944 n/a	1963	1963–66/GAZ-21 1966–68/GAZ-30
MiG-21FL	233	1961	1961–65/GAZ-21*
MiG-21R	448	1964	1966–71/GAZ-21
MiG-21S	145	1964	1966–68/GAZ-21
MiG-21SM	349	1967	1968–71/GAZ-21
MiG-21SMT	281	1970	1971–73/GAZ-21
MiG-21M	n/a	1968	1968–71/GAZ-30**
MiG-21MF	n/a 231	1970	1971–73/GAZ-30** 1975–76/GAZ-21
MiG-21MT	15	1971	1971/GAZ-30
MiG-21bis	2,013	1971	1972–85/GAZ-21
MiG-21U	180 230-plus	1960	1962–66/GAZ-31 1964–68/GAZ-30
MiG-21US	347	1965	1966–70/GAZ-31
MiG-21UM	1,133	1968	1970–85/GAZ-31

* Supplied as component knocked-down kits for local assembly at HAL Nasik in India
** The total number of the manufactured MiG-21Ms and MiG-21MFs at GAZ-30 is about 1,500.

MAIN MiG-21 VERSIONS, MODIFICATIONS AND PROJECTS

MiG-21PF radar-equipped all-weather interceptor

The MiG-21P was the first all-weather interceptor derivative of the Fishbed family, equipped with the RP-21 air-intercept radar. (Mikoyan & Gurevich Design Bureau via author)

The MiG-21PF was the first production-standard all-weather interceptor derivative of the Fishbed family, equipped with the RP-21 Sapfir-21 air-intercept radar and sporting a series of fuselage and powerplant improvements. It was originally designed as an integral component of the MiG-21P-13 air-intercept system (P standing for Perekhvatchik – interceptor – and the number 13 standing for the K-13 missile system with the R-3S heat-seeking missile), launched by a Council of Ministers decree dated 24 July 1958 and the subsequent GKAT order dated 2 August 1958. Both of these government authorizations called for development of an all-weather (i.e. capable of operating at night and in adverse weather) interceptor, based on the MiG-21F design. The fighter and its weapons-control system were required to be submitted for state flight testing in the fourth quarter of 1959. The test and evaluation process had to use two developmental aircraft, each equipped with the new TsD-30 search-and-track airborne radar set and armed with two R-3S heat-seeking missiles.

The design work was completed in early 1959 and the new Fishbed derivative, bearing the prototype designation Ye-7, introduced a vastly modified fuselage with a longer nose and a much larger intake centrebody accommodating the large radar antenna measuring 500mm in diameter, while at the same time retaining the airflow rates of 65kg/sec required for the normal engine operation. The dielectric nose cone was installed with an axis pointing 3° downwards relative to the aircraft's longitudinal axis in order to provide maximum pressure recovery at high AoA. The large parabolic antenna was housed inside the notably enlarged nose cone that moved continuously forward and aft to provide optimum engine working conditions at different speeds and altitudes.

This new Fishbed derivative dispensed with the cannon armament altogether in a bid to compensate for the weight increase caused by the radar installation but retain the performance as per the technical specification. The bulky and heavy ASP-5ND gunsight was replaced by the much simpler and lighter PKI-1 collimator gunsight to enable bomb and napalm tank drops, as well as rocket firings and visual aiming of the R-3S missiles when the radar was switched off. Other avionics components included the RSIU-5V UHV radio, ARK-54I ADF, MRP-56I marker radio receiver, KSI-1 heading system, SRO-2M IFF transponder and the SOD-57M air traffic control transponder. The interceptor prototype also received the KAP-1 single-axis autopilot providing authority in the roll axis.

In order to improve operability from non-paved airfields, the Ye-7 received the new KT-50/2 main wheels with larger tyres, 800mm in diameter, which in turn necessitated larger main undercarriage bays and associated wheel bay doors. The Ye-7 also introduced a simplified airbrake design, and fuselage frames 25 and 28 were modified for attachment of jet-assisted take-off (JATO) rockets.

The interceptor was designed from the outset to cope with fast, high-altitude targets; in addition to the radar it boasted dedicated guidance equipment, represented by the Lasour-1 integrated onboard automated system to receive intercept information, datalinked from the ground control station of the Vozdukh-1 intercept operations control system. Intercept commands (such as heading, altitude and speed), generated by the system's analogue computer, were received by the Lasour-1 equipment and displayed on the respective instruments using bugs (special moving markers on the instruments scale, showing to the pilot where he has to position the indicating needle for altitude, speed, etc.). Lamps were used to issue discrete commands such as afterburner on, zoom climb, and switching on the radar when entering into the terminal attack phase. This way, the Ye-7 pilot was required simply to follow the visual cues to fly a covert – i.e. without use of voice commands from the ground – intercept profile in order to achieve an initial attack position for switching on the radar at a distance of 10km, preferably astern of and slightly below the assigned target.

In 1958 and 1959 OKB-155 rolled out three interceptor prototypes; the first of these, designated as the Ye-7/1, took to the air for the first time on 10 August 1959 in the capable hands of Mikoyan test pilot Piotr Ostapenko. It had ballast in place of the radar and was almost fully dedicated to testing the new inlet design. The Ye-7/1, however, had a very short life as it was lost only three months after its first flight, on 28 November 1959, due to a supersonic stall and the subsequent spin, caused by the loss of directional stability at the maximum permissible Mach number, but the test pilot Igor Kravtsov managed to eject safely. The reason for the loss of directional stability was attributed to the notably altered nose fuselage shape with a large centrebody, the changes having created an additional lateral force at high speed which, in turn, caused the aircraft to yaw excessively and depart from controlled flight.

A Soviet Air Force MiG-21PF seen in a diving attack, unleashing 57mm rockets against ground targets. (Author – *Aviatsia i Kosmonavtika*)

The second prototype, the Ye-7/2, flown for the first time on 1 February 1960, also by OKB-155's Piotr Ostapenko, featured a set of aerodynamic modifications introduced in a bid to improve directional stability, such as an increased-area fin, a ventral fin and the KAP-1 autopilot. The Ye-7/2 was dedicated to testing the TsD-30 radar set but also proved to be a short-lived aircraft; just like the Ye-7/1, it was lost while undergoing its factory flight-test programme. While on its 72nd flight on 5 June 1960, the Ye-7/2 suffered engine failure and was destroyed in the subsequent attempt to land with a flamed-out engine. It touched down 200m before the runway end, and test pilot Igor Kravtsov was lucky to survive the crash.

The Ye-7/3, powered by the uprated R-11F2-300 engine with a maximum afterburner rating of 60.03kN (13,464lb st), took to the air for the first time in May 1960 and was more successful than its two predecessors. In addition to the uprated engine, it introduced a modified tail-end as well as a broader fin, which by 1961 became the production standard, while the brake parachute housing was relocated to the base of the fin, just above the jet pipe. The nose wheel steering mechanism was deleted and the aircraft received a dorsal fuel tank at the rear of the cockpit. The Ye-7/3 was used for initial testing of the TsD-30 radar and the Lasour datalink, operating against real-world airborne targets. It also tested an improved version of the radar, designated as the TsD-30T, which could provide target range information necessary for calculating the R-3S missile's launch envelope (i.e. maximum and minimum permissible launch ranges at different closure speeds and altitudes).

The Ye-7/4, also powered by the uprated R-11F2-300, dispensed with the nose wheel steering, incorporated an enlarged fin and introduced the new KAP-2 autopilot, operating in the roll axis only, while the pitot boom was relocated to a new position atop the inlet and on the centreline. The Ye-7/4 also added a new dorsal tank and wing tanks, housing an additional 380 litres of jet fuel.

The Ye-7/4 prototype was also earmarked to test the further improved TsD-30TP radar and commenced its factory flight tests in August 1960. Together with the Ye-7/3, which was modified in the same fashion, it was used for completing the Ye-7's state testing programme, which finally began on 30 June 1961. In the course of the factory and state testing programmes, the Ye-7/3 logged 160 flights, while the Ye-7/4 added 154 more. The state testing effort, undertaken by the NII-VVS together with OKB-155, was completed in late July 1961.

The maximum speed recorded by the Ye-7 was 2,175km/h, the practical ceiling was 19,000m (62,300ft), while range proved to be 1,600km with two R-3S missiles and internal fuel and 1,900km with a centreline drop tank. Flight endurance in level flight at 19,000m (62,300ft) on internal fuel was 8 minutes, extending to 12 minutes when using a centreline drop tank. Maximum flight endurance at optimum speed and altitude with a drop tank reached 2hrs 27min. Take-off run and landing-roll lengths, demonstrated during the tests, accounted for 850m and 900m respectively. At the same time, the Ye-7's landing speed increased to between 260 and 290km/h, making this phase of flight rather difficult for average-skilled pilots. For intercept operations above 12,000m (39,000ft), pilots were required to wear the VKK-4 pressure suit and GSh-4M pressure helmet.

The radar-equipped interceptor initially received the new in-service designation MiG-21P, and its production was launched at GAZ-21, following a GKAT decision dated March 1960; but it was very soon superseded by the improved MiG-21PF version, featuring an additional 170-litre tank on the top of the fuselage, just behind the cockpit, as well as two 105-litre tanks in the wings. The first production-standard MiG-21PF fighter took to the air on 28 June 1961, and in December that year it received the improved TsD-30TP radar (designated as the RP-21 when installed on the series-production MiG-21PF). This air-intercept radar set boasted better protection against passive jamming (chaff) and non-synchronized pulse jamming, created from other working radars in close proximity and emitting on the same wavelength. The TsD-30TP radar also featured roll-axis stabilization and an increased-size scope in the cockpit.

Other modifications, incorporated in the first series-production fighters (designated as the MiG-21PF but bearing the internal OKB-155 designation Type 76), included a reduction in the volume of the dorsal tank by some 80 litres (due to the larger 'black boxes' of the new radar), provision for using the K-51 weapons system with the RS-2US (AA-1 *Alkali*) AAM, and introduction of the SRZO-2M IFF interrogator/transponder system.

In March 1962 the MiG-21PF received a further improved sub-version of the TsD-30TP radar and was used to test-fire RS-2US missiles; the trials programme, completed in September 1962, proved that the beam-riding missile could be used as an all-weather weapon, replacing the R-3S in bad-weather intercepts. The 15th aircraft from the 16th production batch was the first to be equipped to fire the RS-2US.

As many as 30 MiG-21PFs were rolled out at GAZ-21 in 1961 and 60 more followed suit in the first 10 months of 1962. The MiG-21PF's sub-variants, destined for export customers, were produced at GAZ-30 in Moscow between 1964 and 1968.

MiG-21PFS with blown flaps

The Ye-7SPS was another improved prototype of the radar-equipped interceptor, featuring the new SPS blown flaps system (boundary layer blower) which provided a useful increase in lift during landing approach. The SPS was installed on a production-standard MiG-21PF (Ye-7S c/n 0725) which was then handed over to OKB-155 for testing purposes. The new version was powered by the R-11F2S-300 engine, rated at 60.76kN (13,640lb st), which was modified to supply bleed air in the slot in front of the simple hinged flaps. The new interceptor version, designated as the Ye-7SPS, also introduced the RV-UV radar altimeter and an increased-area brake parachute, the latter housed inside a cylindrical fairing at the base of the rudder. The new brake parachute was cleared for deployment before touchdown to further shorten the aircraft's landing roll.

The modified MiG-21PF, featuring the SPS system, underwent its state testing with the NII-VVS in the first half of 1962. The blown flaps bestowed a notable improvement in landing performance: in combination with the more effective cruciform brake parachute, this novelty enabled the landing roll to be shortened to 480m, while the landing speed decreased to 249km/h. A significant reduction in the take-off run was achieved by use of two SPRD-99 assisted take-off solid-fuel boosters, each developing 24.52kN (5,500lb st) of thrust for 10–17 seconds.

The improved interceptor derivative with SPS system was designated as the MiG-21PFS (Ye-7SPS, Type 94) and entered series production at GAZ-21 in 1962. During the production run the MiG-21PFS received a plethora of additional improvements, such as a larger nose wheel and more effective

B MIG-21 PROFILES

1. The Soviet Air Force's big-spine MiG-21SMTs with extended range, operating during the 1970s and 1980s with the fighter regiments, had a secondary and rather important nuclear attack role, carrying one bomb under the fuselage and featuring a nuclear-attack control panel in the cockpit.

2. North Korea's MiG-21PFMs have survived into the 2010s. Although widely considered as hopelessly obsolete, these small and fast fighters are still maintained in airworthy status and remain a dangerous hit-and-run weapon.

3. The Malian Air Force has on strength two MiG-21UM two-seaters, acquired second-hand from the Czech Republic in the mid-2000s, and these continued sporadic flight operations until the early 2010s.

4. The Soviet Air Force operated a large number of MiG-21US two-seaters in the flight training schools in the 1970s, with their SPS blown flaps system deactivated; a feature that was also the case for the MiG-21PFM single-seaters used for advanced and weapons employment training.

1

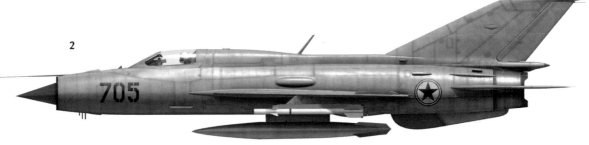

2

3

4

braking system, as well as a still broader-chord tail fin, extending forward a further 450mm to further improve directional stability at high speeds.

The check-flight trials, undertaken by the NII-VVS in 1965, revealed that the MiG-21PFS' maximum range had decreased beyond the permitted 3 per cent tolerance as foreseen by the Soviet Air Force's technical specification – i.e. it fell from 1,550km to 1,300km – while the practical ceiling decreased from 19,000m (62,300ft) to 18,050–18,250m (59,200–59,860ft), depending on the individual aircraft that were tested. The main reason for this performance deterioration was attributed to the increased fuel consumption of the improved engine, combined with a number of airframe alterations and the added weight of the new avionics and equipment, accounting for 70–160kg, while the internal fuel capacity was reduced by about 150 litres.

MiG-21PFM

The MiG-21PFM combined the MiG-21PFS' basic design with the new KM-1 (SK-3) ejection seat, and this was the definitive configuration retained on all subsequent Fishbed derivatives. The new version had a two-piece canopy with fixed windscreen and sideways-hinged (to starboard) main section, instead of the MiG-21PF/PFS' single-piece canopy which acted as a blast shield during ejection. The introduction of a considerably simpler and therefore more dependable ejection system was made due to reliability concerns regarding the complex SK-2 system, which had a large number of mechanisms and pyrotechnical cartridges in order to form a blast shield, separate the pilot from the seat at the appropriate moment and deploy the rescue parachute. The new KM-1 crew escape system enabled safe ejections at zero altitude and a minimum speed of 130km/h during take-off run and landing roll. The new ejection seat was used for the first time on the Ye-7M, which entered production under the MiG-21PFM designation but still bearing the internal designation Type 94. This new derivative also had its internal fuel capacity reduced by some 100 litres compared to that of the initial-production MiG-21PF. In the 1970s a proportion of MiG-21PFMs had their R-11F2S-300 engines replaced by the more powerful R-13-300.

The Ye-7M was submitted for its state flight testing on 29 December 1962 and was used for trialling the new K-51 guided missile system with the RS-2US radar beam-riding missile. The new derivative successfully completed its state flight tests in 1964 and was recommended for entry into service with the Soviet Air Force.

The MiG-21PFM was a further refined interceptor derivative with better radar and a vastly improved landing performance, but still retaining the weak armament of only two short-range AAMs. (Author's collection)

The MiG-21PF/PFS/PFM's time to intercept a target flying at 16,000m (52,500ft) was 8 minutes from the initial take-off run. A manoeuvring limitation of 3.5G was imposed during the early years of MiG-21PF/PFM operations, due to radar operability and reliability concerns over the vacuum tube technology, but by the early 1970s this restriction had been lifted and the interceptor was cleared for manoeuvring with up to 8.5G depending on the fuel state and external stores. Owing to their weak armament of only two short-range AAMs, both the MiG-21PF and PFM variants were nicknamed the 'Peaceful Doves' in the Soviet Union and Warsaw Pact.

The MiG-21PF/PFS/PFM was in production at GAZ-21 for the Soviet Air Force between 1961 and 1968.

MiG-21PF/PFM's export versions

Derivatives of the MiG-21PF/PFM/FL for export were produced at GAZ-30 between 1964 and 1968, with peak rates of 30 aircraft a month. The aircraft supplied to the Warsaw Pact countries and some other close allies of the Soviet Union featured an equipment/avionics configuration close to that of their Soviet counterparts, known as the A-variant of the respective Fishbed derivative (i.e. Type 94A or MiG-21PFMA). The MiG-21PF variant exported to Vietnam was close to the A-variant but had some minor design differences (an ARK-10 ADF without range calculator and an improved KSI-2 heading system) and received the MiG-21PFV designation.

The derivative sold to a number of developing countries was designated as the MiG-21FL and featured a considerably 'sanitized' avionics suite; this primarily concerned the radar, designated as the R-1L (export version of the TsD-30T) but replaced in 1965 by the R-2L (export version of the TsD-30TP), which lacked some of the operational modes of the original radars used by the Soviet Air Force and had somewhat reduced detection ranges.

Bearing the internal design bureau designation Type 77, the MiG-21FL, powered by the R-11F-300 engine, featured the MiG-21PF's SK ejection seat and upwards-opening canopy, plus the smaller (later enlarged) fin. It lacked the Lasour datalink as well as the RS-2US missile and S-24 rocket capability. The radar installed on Indian Air Force MiG-21FLs was the R-2L and the radio was an improved RSIU-5T version, but no Soviet-made IFF was supplied as this system was installed locally in India. The MiG-21FL was flight-tested for the first time in the second half of 1963 and the following year it underwent its state testing and evaluation with the NII-VVS. This derivative was also produced under licence in India by Hindustan Aeronautics Limited (HAL) at Nasik, using component knocked-down kits supplied by GAZ-21. A number of MiG-21FLs assembled at GAZ-21 were operated by the Soviet Air Force and the type was exported to a number of developing states such as Algeria, Afghanistan, Egypt, Iraq and Syria.

MiG-21R for tactical recce missions

The MiG-21R (Type 94R; NATO codename: Fishbed-H) was a MiG-21PFM derivative tailored for tactical reconnaissance, but which retained the full all-weather interceptor capability of its predecessor. Its development was launched following the Council of Ministers decree issued in October 1963 and the subsequent GKAT order dated 19 November 1963. The airframe/ powerplant design was originally based on that of the MiG-21PF with minimum alterations, with the reconnaissance-gathering mission equipment housed in a large underfuselage pod carried on the centreline pylon. The MiG-21R was able to carry underwing drop tanks, which further increased the fuel capacity and extended mission radius.

The MiG-21R was the first member of the Fishbed family to introduce four underwing pylons, modified to carry additional fuel tanks for extending range when the aircraft was operating with the large underfuselage pod housing specialized recce equipment. (Author's collection)

YE-8 – THE RADICALLY REWORKED INTERCEPTOR

A Ye-8 programme was formally launched in 1960, following a Council of Ministers decree dated 30 May which tasked OKB-155 to commence design of a radically improved MiG-21PF derivative to be equipped with the all-new S-23 weapons control system. Designated as the Ye-8, it was to include the all-new Sapfir-23 air-intercept radar and the K-23 AAM, featuring semi-active radar homing and infrared homing derivatives. Due to the large diameter of the radar antenna's reflecting dish, the Ye-8's nose was completely redesigned to house the radar, while the inlet was moved under the forward fuselage and fitted with sharp-edged lips swept-back at 55° in plan view. The aircraft's aerodynamics were also improved by adding foreplanes, also known as destabilizers, which were 2.6m in span. Installed horizontally just below the fuselage centreline, these foreplanes freely pivoted in subsonic flight, remaining aligned with the local airflow, while in supersonic flight they locked into neutral position, causing a two-fold increase in lift at Mach 2 and moving the lift vector forward, resulting in improved supersonic manoeuvrability. At 15,000m (49,200ft) the new aerodynamic feature enabled a maximum sustained turn with 5G load factor (in such conditions, the production-standard MiG-21 was limited to 2G only). In order to improve the supersonic directional stability, the ventral fin was considerably enlarged; it

hinged sideways when the undercarriage was in the extended position, and was stowed horizontally towards the right.

The Ye-8 also introduced integral fuel tanks without flexible cells, occupying five compartments in the fuselage and four in the wings, with a total volume of 3,200 litres; there was also provision for carriage of a 600-litre centreline tank. The cockpit was set to introduce the then new KM-1 ejection seat, with the canopy featuring a fixed forward section and a movable rear section hinged to starboard. The Ye-8 introduced a new engine, the R-21F-300, a vastly improved derivative of the R-11F-300, featuring an increased-diameter compressor inlet to supply greater airflow in order to achieve increased thrust ratings. It also sported a new afterburner design, with convergent/divergent multi-flap nozzle, which projected well beyond the rear of the fuselage. The new engine had a slightly increased weight and its rating at military and afterburner power settings increased to 46.2kN (10,362 lb st) and 70.60kN (15,873lb st) respectively.

The Ye-8's wings, main undercarriage legs, fin and tailplanes were inherited unchanged from the MiG-21PF, with the tailplanes mounted 135mm lower. The radically reworked prototype introduced a new taller and stronger nose undercarriage leg which retracted to the rear and was provided with a larger tyre and new brake unit;

the main undercarriage legs were also equipped with larger tyres and boasted improved brakes.

The Ye-8/1 was the first prototype of the radically reworked Fishbed version, lacking the radar and the KM-1 ejection seat (replaced by the MiG-21PF's original SK seat but without blast protection for the pilot). It made its maiden flight on 17 April 1962 with Georgii Mosolov at the controls. The test effort, however, turned out to be a rather problematic undertaking after the fourth flight due to engine problems, such as frequent compressor stalls and flame-outs. During 40 test flights the R-21F-300 experienced no fewer than 11 flame-outs (with subsequent mid-air restarts), and the engine had to be changed twice – after the 21st and 25th flights. While on the 40th flight on 11 September 1962, during supersonic acceleration at 10,000m (32,800ft), flying straight and level at Mach 1.7, the Ye-8/1 experienced an uncontained engine failure at the sixth compressor stage. Parts of the disintegrated disc caused severe damage to the starboard wing, both hydraulic systems and the fuel tanks, resulting in an onboard fire and rapid roll with violent deceleration. The pilot managed to eject but barely survived, having sustained numerous injures from the airflow after ejecting and receiving additional injures upon impact with the ground, which resulted in Mosolov spending more than a year in hospital.

The second prototype, designated as the Ye-8/2, also lacked the radar but featured blown flaps, missile pylons and a plethora of other improvements. It took to the air on 29 June 1962 and by 4 September the same year had amassed 13 successful test flights in the capable hands of OKB-155 test pilot Alexander Fedotov. The Ye-8/2 demonstrated a practical ceiling of 19,650m (64,450ft) and a maximum speed of 2,050km/h at 15,000m (49,200ft).

The Ye-8/1's crash, however, combined with the unreliable and still immature engine, eventually put an end to this otherwise promising programme; later, the Ye-8/2 was utilized as a ground test platform for a number of novel design features intended for the newly developed (in the mid-1960s) MiG-23 swing-wing fighter.

ABOVE The radically reworked Ye-8 interceptor prototype had a large radar antenna, an underfuselage intake and a more powerful R-21-300 turbojet, but was plagued by powerplant troubles during the early stages of its flight-test programme. These problems eventually caused the loss of the first prototype, the Ye-8/1, on 11 September 1962. (Mikoyan & Gurevich Design Bureau via author)

The MiG-21R became the first Fishbed version to feature four underwing hardpoints instead of the two on all previous MiG-21s; all the hardpoints were plumbed for carriage of 490-litre drop tanks or two tanks and two R-3S AAMs for self-defence.

The first two prototypes of the reconnaissance Fishbed, which received the new prototype designation Ye-7R, were manufactured at GAZ-21 at Gorkii in cooperation with OKB-155 (renamed in 1966 as MMZ Zenith), using production-standard MiG-21PF airframes. The new derivative was initially designated as the MiG-21PR and the first prototype took to the air in 1964. The following year, both the MiG-21PRs were submitted for their state testing effort with the NII-VVS. Series production at GAZ-21 was launched in 1965, with the first production-standard aircraft, eventually designated as the MiG-21R (c/n 030101), being rolled out in early 1966. The type stayed in production at GAZ-21 in Gorkii until 1971.

A wider 340-litre dorsal tank was introduced on the production-standard MiG-21R, an addition that marginally increased the aerodynamic drag while increasing the internal fuel capacity to 2,800 litres. The MiG-21R also sported the MiG-21PFM's broad fin and the cruciform brake parachute, the latter housed in a pod at the base of the fin. The aircraft was also the first member of the Fishbed family to receive an AoA sensor on the starboard side of the fuselage, it being used to feed information to the newly introduced AP-155 three-axis full-authority autopilot and also to an AoA indicator in the cockpit, while the PVD-5 pitot boom, located above the nose, was moved to the right for better pilot visibility. A back-up pitot probe was installed in front of the cockpit on the starboard side.

The MiG-21R retained the RP-21M air-intercept radar and added an SPO-3 radar warning receiver (RWR) with 360-degree coverage in the horizontal plane. Its receiver antennas were housed in small cylindrical pods on the wingtips, while the 'black boxes' were housed in the underfuselage pod and the indicator was installed in the cockpit. From 1969, all newly produced MiG-21Rs received the Ts-27AMSh rear-view periscope, fitted on the top of the moving part of the canopy; earlier aircraft received the periscope as a retrofit.

The MiG-21R retained the entire air-to-air and air-to-ground ordnance selection of its predecessor, the MiG-21PFM, except for the GP-9 gun-pod. The reconnaissance Fishbed had, however, a reduced manoeuvring limitation (from 8.5G to 6G) because of the four underwing drop tanks and the sensitive electronic equipment housed in the centreline pod. Furthermore, its maximum speed at high altitude was reduced to 1,700km/h, equating to Mach 1.6; this limitation was imposed in order to maintain enough directional stability when equipped with the underfuselage pod and underwing tanks, thus avoiding unwanted oscillations in yaw that resulted in poor-quality photographs. The MiG-21R was required to take off in afterburner mode only due to the heavier configuration than that of its fighter predecessors.

Another reconnaissance version, dubbed MiG-21RF, was purposely built for Egypt; it lacked the reconnaissance pod and featured an internally mounted pack of three A-39 cameras on a common frame located under the cockpit and covered by a sideways-hinged panel with camera windows.

MiG-21R's reconnaissance pods

There were no fewer than four versions of the MiG-21R's reconnaissance pod, designated as the D-, N-, R- and T-series, designed for daylight photo-reconnaissance, night-time photo-reconnaissance, electronic intelligence (ELINT) and TV-reconnaissance respectively; in addition, there was a dedicated pod for radiation contamination monitoring.

The R-series of ELINT pods were equipped with the SRS-6 and the SRS-7M or the Romb-4A and Romb-4B ELINT systems and a single AFA-39 camera. Its sub-version, supplied in the late 1960s to Warsaw Pact allies, incorporated a single AFA-39 camera, installed in a forward oblique position, and the Romb-4A and Romb-4B systems for intercepting radar and communication electronic emissions, recorded on MS-81 wire recorders, while the ASO-2I chaff/flare dispensers were used for self-defence.

The D-series of daylight photo-reconnaissance pods weighted some 285kg and contained a battery of six AFA-39 cameras and one AShTShAFA-SM camera. One of the AFA-39 cameras was installed forward-facing in the pod's nose, while the other six were vertically mounted. The AFA-39 (A-39), equipped with a 100mm focal-length lens and using 80mm-wide film, was the most-widely used Soviet camera in the 1950s, 1960s and 1970s. It captured a swathe the width of which was 0.7 times the altitude of the carrier aircraft when vertically mounted; two times when obliquely mounted. The length of the photographed swathe in continuous operation was 120 and 180 times the carrier aircraft's altitude, respectively. The D-series pod also housed an SPO-3R RWR and two ASO-2I countermeasures dispensers, usually loaded with PRP-2I-15 chaff cartridges.

The N-series pods for night-time photo-reconnaissance were equipped with one UA-47 camera featuring two lenses, inclined at 160° left and right, and 152 FP-100 illumination flares. The camera was operated at between 300 and 1,000m (980 and 3,300ft) while the aircraft was flying at between 750 and 1,100km/h; the 80mm-wide film was enough for shooting 152 pairs of frames.

The T-series of pods were equipped with the Barii-M TV-reconnaissance system and were used only by the Soviet Air Force, operating in conjunction with a truck-mounted ground receiver station for real-time reception of the video image.

The MiG-21R's radiation monitoring pod was equipped with the Yeir-1M system for taking air samples and detecting particulate constituents when flying in contaminated atmospheres.

MiG-21S

The MiG-21S (Type 95) was another tactical fighter version of the Fishbed. Its development commenced in 1963 following the Council of Ministers decree issued in the first half of 1962, with a requirement that the development phase be completed in a little more than three years. During that time, Vimpel Design Bureau was tasked to develop the vastly improved R-13M heat-seeking missile, derived from the R-3S. The first MiG-21S prototype entered flight testing in late 1963, and in 1964 it was joined by another example: one of these was based on the MiG-21PF and the other on the MiG-21PFM; both were subsequently handed over to undergo state testing and evaluation with the NII-VVS in 1964.

The MiG-21S featured the MiG-21R's basic airframe with four underwing pylons. The enlarged dorsal tank gave a straight line from the top of the canopy to the front of the fin, while the pitot boom above the air intake was

The RP-22M Sapfir radar, installed for the first time on the MiG-21S, used a twist-Cassegrain antenna with monopulse target-tracking instead of conical scan. (Author)

offset to starboard. In order to be more capable of operating from unpaved runways, the new derivative also received a strengthened undercarriage.

The MiG-21S retained the R-11F2S-300 engine and the AP-155 autopilot with automatic levelling capability, engaged in the event of pilot disorientation. The most important new component, incorporated into the MiG-21S' new mission suite, was the vastly improved RP-22S Sapfir-21 air-intercept radar, using a twist-Cassegrain antenna and featuring the monopulse target direction-finding method. This method provided notably better resistance to both passive and active jamming compared to the conical scanning, as used by the RP-21MA. The RP-22S was a more powerful system which boasted some 150 per cent greater target detection and tracking range compared to that of its predecessor. Bomber-type targets were typically detected at 30km and tracked at 15km, while against fighter-size targets the RP-22S' maximum detection range reached 18km and tracking range was up to 11km. The RP-22S' analogue processor calculated the minimum and maximum R-3S/R-3R launch ranges depending on the altitude and closing speed, generating the 'launch permitted' and 'break' commands. The new radar was also capable of supporting limited side-on (high-aspect) intercepts, something not possible with the RP-21MA as it was optimized for tail-on intercepts only.

The new radar was introduced together with the new R-3R (AA-2B) semi-active radar homing (SARH) missile which had a range of 0.8–7km; it was used for all-weather intercepts and was suitable against non-manoeuvrable targets. After launch, the fighter was free to manoeuvre within a limited space, keeping the target within the radar's gumball limits (30° up/down and left/right) as the R-3R homed onto the reflected signal from the target, continuously tracked by the RP-22S. The radar's rangefinding function provided the pilot with information about the maximum and minimum missile launch ranges at different altitudes and closing speeds (displayed on a mechanical needle display on the ASP-PF-21 gunsight). It also supplied range information for the employment of the GSh-23L 23mm cannon against air targets and for firing both the gun and rockets against ground targets. The SPO-10 Sirena-2 RWR was also incorporated into the mission suite of MiG-21S aircraft. It had antennas looking back from the top of the fin; and the cockpit indicator provided the rough direction of any radars 'painting' the aircraft, with 45° precision in azimuth.

The gunsight was the new ASP-PF-21 lead-computing gyro unit, enabling more precise firing against air targets with the GSh-23L cannon (carried in the GP-9 conformal gun-pod) as well as generating better aiming information for using the cannon, rockets and bombs against ground and sea targets. The gunsight, however, 'toppled' at 2.75G, thus limiting the ability to aim the GSh-23L cannon in a high-G turning dogfight. The MiG-21S also incorporated an improved Lasour-M datalink for receiving steering commands from a ground-based intercept control station.

The armament of this vastly improved Fishbed derivative was enhanced in 1974 with the addition of the R-13M (K-13M, NATO AA-2C) heat-seeking missile, an enhanced derivative of the R-3S missile incorporating a more-sensitive nitrogen-cooled infrared seeker and boasting better agility and extended range; it also bestowed some reduced manoeuvring limitations on the launch platform. The MiG-21S was the first Fishbed derivative capable of carrying a total of four AAMs – typically a combination of two R-3Ss or two R-13Ms and two R-3Rs, or two missiles on the inner pylons and two 490-litre drop tanks on the outer pylons.

The MiG-21M was the export derivative of the MiG-21S; a heavier version with four underwing weapon pylons and the first member of the Fishbed family to feature the ventral GSh-23L cannon with 200 rounds. (Author's collection)

The MiG-21S was also capable of using the IVP-2 Samotsver forward-looking infrared sensor, which was integrated with the radar and the ASP-PF-21 gunsight. Detection range against a twin-engine medium bomber was between 4 and 12km, depending on altitude, aspect and the operating mode of the target's engines.

The new Fishbed derivative entered series production at GAZ-21 in 1965, and the plant rolled out an initial batch of 25 aircraft in the same year, even before completion of the type's state flight testing programme. The MiG-21S remained in production until 1968.

MiG-21M

The MiG-21S' export derivative, designated as the MiG-21M (Type 96), was the first member of the Fishbed family to receive the 23mm GSh-23L built-in cannon, housed in a neat ventral pack between frames 11 and 16 and provided with 200 rounds in a belt around the fuselage. The MiG-21M also incorporated an improved ASP-PF gunsight, together with an SSh-45-1-100S camera-gun, but retained the MiG-21PFM's RP-21M downgraded conical-scan radar since the more advanced RP-22S system was not yet cleared for export. The MiG-21 underwent its state testing and evaluation programme with the NII-VVS in 1968; that same year the first nine examples were rolled out at GAZ-30 in Moscow. The type was in production until 1971, while in India its local assembly was carried out between 1973 and 1981 under the designation 'Type 88'.

MiG-21SM/MF

The MiG-21SM (Type 95M; later redesignated Type 15) and its export derivative MiG-21MF (Type 96F) inherited the MiG-21S' basic airframe and systems, combined with the new R-13-300 turbojet. This engine was a follow-on development of the R-11-300-series with increased thrust, developing 65.33kN (14,652lb st) at maximum afterburner rating and 39.93kN (8,973lb st) at military power rating, and featured a fully variable afterburner. It was standard procedure to use about half afterburner for take-off to conserve fuel. The new engine weighed 1,135kg.

The MiG-21MF, which entered production in the late 1960s, was the export derivative of the MiG-21SM. It was widely exported and saw a lot of combat in local conflicts worldwide. (Author)

THE MiG-21FL

The Indian Air Force was the main customer for the MiG-21FL, a tailor-made export version of the MiG-21PFM that retained some features from the MiG-21PF, such as the forward-hinged canopy. It was equipped with a downgraded radar, and could not use the RS-2US beam-riding missile and 240mm rockets. The Indian Air Force was the first air arm to enhance the weapons suite of the interceptor derivatives of the Fishbed with the GP-9 conformal gun-pod, containing one GSh-23L 23mm cannon with 200 rounds.

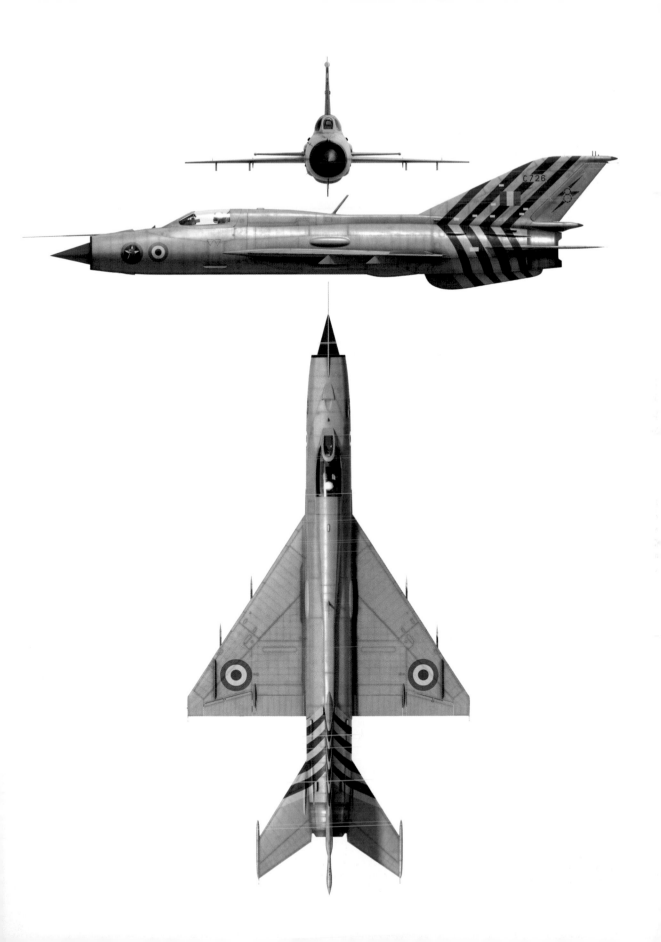

The MiG-21SM and MF derivatives can be easily distinguished from the gun-armed MiG-21M thanks to the presence of small deflector plates installed under the auxiliary engine inlet. The underwing pylons also received the BD3-6021D adaptor beams for carrying the MBD-2-67 multiple bomb racks and the UB-32M 32-round rocket packs. During the 1980s the weapons control system of many of the exported MiG-21MF aircraft was modified to give it the capability of firing the highly agile R-60 and R-60MK AAMs.

The MiG-21SM/MF also received a rear-view periscope, fitted on top of the canopy, and the new PVD-7 pitot boom with vanes for AoA and sideslip angle measurement, used to provide data for precise gun-aiming calculations. The mission suite also included the SPO-10 Sirena-3M RWR, SRO-2 IFF transponder, SRZO-2 interrogator-transponder, SOD-57 ATC transponder and the Lasour-M datalink equipment. The MiG-21MFs built for use by the air arms of both the Warsaw Pact and developing countries continued to be equipped with an export version of the old RP-21MA radar.

Both the MiG-21SM and MiG-21MF featured a built-in GSh-23L gun-pack and an improved ASP-PFD-21 gunsight. The internal fuel tanks had a total capacity of 2,650 litres.

The MiG-21SM made its maiden flight in 1967 and remained in production at GAZ-21 in Gorkii for the Soviet Air Force between 1968 and 1974. Production of the MiG-21MF for export customers began at GAZ-30 in Moscow in 1969 and continued until 1974; in the first year of manufacture as many as 96 examples were rolled out, all of which were promptly exported to Egypt. Between 1974 and 1976 the MiG-21MF was also produced at GAZ-21 in Gorkii, where a total of 231 of the type were built.

MiG-21SMT/MT

The MiG-21SMT (Type 50) was a derivative with a massively increased internal fuel capacity, reaching 3,100 litres, while the MiG-21MT was its export derivative with a sanitized mission suite. Both introduced very large dorsal spines which extended from the cockpit to halfway along the fin and then tapered to join up with the parachute housing, and which provided maximum possible tankage. The three-cell dorsal conformal tank package accommodated 900 litres of fuel. In addition, the new R-13F-300 engine received an emergency afterburning mode, rated at 68.08kN (15,268lb st). Flying at low level at speeds close to Mach 1, this new enhanced afterburning mode provided a thrust increase of some 18.59kN (4,180lb), compared to the baseline R-13-300. The MiG-21SMT's take-off weight with full internal tanks and two missiles was 8,900kg, while the maximum take-off weight with air-to-ground ordnance under the wings and a centreline drop tank reached 10,100kg.

Directional stability issues, experienced at high AoA because the considerably enlarged spine distorted airflow around the fin, eventually prompted Mikoyan designers to rework the spine tank, the volume of which was reduced to 600 litres, reducing in turn the total fuel capacity to 2,950 litres. The MiG-21SMTs already produced in 1971 by

The big-spine MiG-21SMT was plagued by some controllability and stability issues due to the huge dorsal spine tank, which disturbed the airflow around the fin at high AoA, but the aircraft proved well suited for use in the low-level nuclear delivery role. (Author)

GAZ-21 in Gorkii retained the original big spine throughout their service life, while the examples assembled in 1972 and 1973 featured a smaller dorsal tank. In total, as many as 281 MiG-21SMTs rolled off the line between 1971 and 1973 (distributed over 15 production series), including 116 big-spine examples.

Only 15 export-standard MiG-21MTs (Type 96T) were produced at GAZ-30 in Moscow in 1971, but these big-spine Fishbeds were never exported and instead were used by the Soviet Air Force, initially by one of the squadrons of the 234th Guards Fighter Regiment at Kubinka for air displays. Later, they were handed over to serve with one of the squadrons of a fighter-bomber regiment stationed in East Germany.

The MiG-21bis was the last of the long Fishbed family line, sporting better equipment, more power and a strengthened airframe optimized for low-level air combat and ground-attack missions. (Author)

MiG-21bis – the last of the line

The MiG-21bis (known also as Ye-7bis and Type 75) was the last mass-produced version of the Fishbed. It was purposely redesigned in order to be better suited for high-G manoeuvring dogfights at low and medium levels, where previous versions had demonstrated a number of shortcomings and were hampered by a plethora of operating limitations in terms of maximum speed and G. This new-style air combat, experienced for the first time in the late 1960s in the Middle East, required from the Fishbed more power, more fuel, better weapons (i.e. missiles able to be launched during high-G manoeuvres) and better sighting systems, as well as improved stability and controllability characteristics and reduced low-level speed restrictions. In the event, the MiG-21bis, developed as a successor to the MiG-21SMT, successfully integrated a 1960s-technology airframe with a 1970s analogue avionics suite and a further uprated powerplant, combined in the mid/late-1970s with modern lightweight dogfight missiles.

The main feature of this last production derivative was the Tumanskii R-25-300 engine, derived from the R-13F-300 and optimized for low-level operations. It was rated at 40.20kN (9,038lb st) dry and 67.20kN (15,653lb st) at full afterburner, increasing to 97kN (21,790lb st) at the emergency afterburner setting, which was permitted for up to 3 minutes at low altitude. Pilots often noted, however, that the more powerful and heavier MiG-21bis was much less agile than the MiG-21F-13 and PF/PFM versions, claiming that the last Fishbed derivative 'behaved like a bull' in the air, while flying the lighter MiG-21PF/PFM was 'like riding a stallion'.

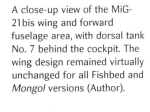

A close-up view of the MiG-21bis wing and forward fuselage area, with dorsal tank No. 7 behind the cockpit. The wing design remained virtually unchanged for all Fishbed and *Mongol* versions (Author).

The MiG-21bis' flight tests showed that the new and considerably more powerful engine significantly boosted the aircraft's low-level performance; for example, the climb rate was improved by some 1.6 times and at Mach 0.9 at low level it reached some 235m/sec with emergency afterburner on. At the same time, the MiG-21bis retained some of the chief design shortcomings of its predecessors, such as the limited operational radius and radar performance, lack of beyond-visual-range missiles, poor pilot visibility (particularly in his 6 o'clock), mediocre slow-speed handling

NUCLEAR FIGHTER-BOMBERS

There were several MiG-21 variants that featured dedicated sub-variants with added-on nuclear capability, distinguished by the letter N (derived from the word *Nositel* – carrier [of a nuclear bomb]) in their type designation. The MiG-21S' nuclear-capable derivative bore the Type 95N designation; MiG-21SM – Type 95MT (or Type 15N); MiG-21SMT – Type 50N; MiG-21M – Type 96N; MiG-21MF – Type 96FN; and the MiG-21bis – Type 75N.

The nuclear-capable Fishbed*s* introduced dedicated wiring to enable use of a single nuclear bomb carried on the centreline pylon, together with a control panel in the cockpit, installed on the top of the fixed windscreen frame. The control panel enabled the pilot to arm the bomb, perform its emergency jettisoning and set the desired type of detonation – airburst or upon impact with the ground. The Soviet Air Force's three-squadron fighter-bomber regiments, stationed in the 1970s and 1980s in East Germany and some other East European counties, had one of their component squadrons permanently equipped for the tactical nuclear role, with the nuclear bomb's control panel always installed. Ground crews regularly practised fitting training rounds, while pilots practised delivery profiles using standard practice bombs.

The nuclear bomb was designed for delivery in either level flight or by the so-called toss-bombing method. The latter called first for acceleration in ultra-level flight at low level to 1,050km/h, then a 45° climb and release of the bomb at about 1,500m (4,920ft), which then impacted the ground some 7km from the release point or detonated in the air at low level in order to deliver a better blast wave destructive effect on surface targets.

There was another, more precise derivative of the toss-bombing method – the so-called over-the-shoulder release – which called for acceleration in level flight to 1,050km/h at 100m (330ft) above the terrain and then commencement of a looping manoeuvre. Bomb release took place when the nose went just beyond the vertical, at a 106° pitch angle, and at an altitude of about 3,000m (9,840ft). In this event, after release the bomb travelled on a ballistic trajectory, initially going sharply upwards and then reversing downwards, hitting the ground immediately beneath the release point. After release, the MiG-21 pilot had 1–2 minutes to escape from the blast wave at full afterburner before the bomb's detonation, at a distance of some 10km.

The RN-28 bomb was the main nuclear weapon carried by Soviet tactical aircraft in the 1970s and 1980s, superseding an earlier design known as the RN-25. A low-yield weapon, the RN-28 was equipped with a programmable control unit that allowed the type of desired detonation – airburst or upon impact with the ground – to be set before take-off, while the bomb's yield was adjustable between 1 and 10 kilotons.

characteristics and high pilot workload during all phases of flight.

Air-to-air ordnance initially consisted of the new R-13M and the R-55 heat-seeking missiles (the latter an RS-2US derivative equipped with a heat-seeking homing head), but in the mid-1970s the R-55 was rapidly superseded by the much better R-60, and eventually the R-60M in the early 1980s. Thanks to the APU-60-2 twin-round launcher rails suspended on the inner pair of underwing pylons, the MiG-21bis was capable of carrying up to six R-60/R-60Ms or a combination of two R-3Rs/R-13Ms and four R-60s. It also retained the GSh-23L internal gun-pack with 200 rounds, later increased to 250 rounds. The aircraft's fuel system was also improved by the introduction of an enlarged dorsal tank package (essentially the same as that installed on the late-production MiG-21SMTs), resulting in an internal fuel capacity of 2,880 litres.

The MiG-21bis airframe incorporated a number of structural changes and was stressed to 8.5G in order to be better suited for low-level dogfighting. The nose inlet diameter was increased to 900mm as opposed to the 870mm for its predecessors, to satisfy the increased airflow requirements of the more powerful R-25-300 engine, but the nose centrebody remained unchanged.

The new Fishbed version retained the RP-22S Sapfir-21S radar with a marginally improved look-down capability and received the improved ASP-PFD-21 gunsight. The MiG-21bis derivative, built for developing countries, was equipped with the old-generation Almaz-23 conical-scan radar, an improved RP-21MA derivative, upgraded to guide R-3R SARH missiles.

A proportion of the production-standard MiG-21bis' also received the Polet-OI flight/navigation suite with the SAU-23ESN automatic flight-control system (incorporating an autopilot with three-axis stabilization capability) and the RSBN-5S tactical navigation and instrument landing system – an important asset in bad-weather operations; particularly so given the MiG-21bis' limited fuel capacity.

There was also a MiG-21bis production-standard sub-variant without the Polet-OI and RSBN-5S systems, but featuring the Lasour-M (ARL-SM) datalink equipment for remotely controlled intercepts. Some aircraft also had an additional gun camera, mounted in a non-standard 'scabbed-on' fairing in the nose, by the side of the PVD-18 pitot boom. There were no different Soviet Air Force designations for these MiG-21bis sub-variants, but that equipped with the RSBN-5S was given the NATO codename Fishbed-N, while the Lasour-M-equipped machine was known as the Fishbed-L.

Two R-13Ms and two pairs of R-60M dogfight missiles, carried on twin-launcher units on the outer pylons, could be employed by the MiG-21bis derivative. (Author)

Design of the MiG-21bis commenced at the Mikoyan Design Bureau in 1971, and in February 1972 it entered service with the Soviet Air Force; as many as 35 aircraft were delivered during the first production year. The MiG-21bis was built at GAZ-21 at Gorkii only; production continued until 1985, with as many as 2,030 examples rolling off the line or delivered in the form of component knocked-down kits for assembly by HAL Nasik in India.

Soviet Air Force examples bore the internal Mikoyan Design Bureau designation Type 75, while the examples built for export to the Warsaw Pact member states were designated as the Type 75A, and those for the developing world were known as the Type 75B. The MiG-21bis was also manufactured under licence in India by HAL Nasik between 1979 and 1987 – as many as 220 examples were assembled there, with a gradually increasing local content of airframe parts and systems; the internal design bureau designation of this specific MiG-21bis sub-variant was Type 75L. Initially, six completed MiG-21bis aircraft were delivered to India, followed by 65 kits for local assembly and finally 220 more were built at HAL in Nasik using locally manufactured parts.

MiG-21bis' heat-seeking air-to-air missiles				
	R-3S	R-13M	R-60	R-60MK
Maximum low-level range/rear quarter	2.5km (1.55 miles)	3.5km (2.17 miles)	2km (1.24 miles)	2.2km (1.37 miles)
Maximum high-level range/rear quarter	7km (4.35 miles)	13km (8.07 miles)	8km (4.97 miles)	8km (4.97 miles)
Minimum range/rear quarter	1km (0.62 miles)	0.9km (0.56 miles)	0.2km (0.12 miles)	0.2km (0.12 miles)
Maximum G of the launch aircraft	2	3.7	7	7
Maximum G of the target	3	5	8	8
All-aspect capability	None	None	None	Limited
Weight	76.6kg (169lb)	90kg (198lb)	43.5kg (96lb)	44kg (97lb)
Warhead weight	11.3kg (24.9lb)	11.3kg (24.9lb)	3kg (6.6lb)	(7.7lb)

The MiG-21U's first prototype, known as the Ye-6U/1, made its maiden flight on 17 October 1960. (Mikoyan & Gurevich Design Bureau via author)

MiG-21 two-seaters

Development work on the MiG-21 two-seater began following the Council of Ministers decree dated 11 November 1959, under the initial OKB-155 designation UTIMiG-21F and factory designation Ye-6U or Type 66. This new version utilized the MiG-21F-13 basic airframe and powerplant and was

A view into the rear cockpit of the MiG-21U, occupied by the instructor who lacked any meaningful forward visibility. (Author's collection)

required to have a 2,000–2,200km/h maximum speed, 20,000m (65,600ft) practical ceiling and 1,400km range on internal fuel. Take-off run with two R-3S missiles was not to exceed 700m and landing roll was to be below 1,200m and 600m, respectively without and with the brake parachute.

The two-seater introduced a redesigned nose section, at frame 18, by inserting the second cockpit (occupied by the instructor) which, as expected, caused a reduction in the internal fuel tankage. In a bid to compensate for this, at least in part, a new flexible tank was added between frames 14 and 22, and consequently the internal fuel volume increased to 2,350 litres.

Both of the MiG-21U cockpits were provided with SK ejection seats lacking the blast protection function; instead the front cockpit had a fixed windscreen, while the single-piece moving main part of the canopy for both cockpits hinged to starboard. The cockpits were separated by a transparent screen and the instructor, sitting in the rear cockpit, had a very poor forward view, especially during take-off and landing.

The two-seater retained the MiG-21F-13's ASP-5ND gyro lead-computing gunsight and the SRD-5 radar rangefinder, but the NR-30 cannon was deleted. Just like the single-seater, the intake centrebody had three working positions – at the rear for flight at speeds below Mach 1.5, in the middle for Mach 1.5 to Mach 1.9, and fully forward at speeds exceeding Mach 1.9. The weapons suite included two R-3S AAMs on underwing pylons and one GP-A-12.7 conformal gun-pod on the centreline housing an A-12.7 12.7mm machine gun with 60 rounds. In the air-to-ground role the two-seater was capable of carrying two free-fall bombs, each weighing up to 500kg, or two 16-round rocket pods on the underwing pylons. The two-seater also retained the provision for using two assisted take-off SPRD-99 rocket boosters.

The main undercarriage units were provided with KT-92 large-diameter (800mm) braking wheels, while the airbrake was of single-piece type, installed on the centreline, and the brake parachute was housed in the underside of the fuselage, between frames 30 and 32. The pitot boom was moved to the centreline position above the nose intake. The MiG-21 two-seater was equipped with the KAP-2 autopilot from the outset, its purpose being to improve stability in the roll axis.

The two-seater's first prototype, designated as the Ye-6U/1, was built in 1960 and made its maiden flight on 17 October the same year in the capable hands of

The MiG-21US improved two-seater featured the R-11F2S-300 engine and blown flaps in order to reduce landing speed. (Author)

42

Mikoyan test pilot Piotr Ostapenko. In March 1961 the Ye-6U/1 was handed over for its state testing and evaluation programme at Akhtubinsk, followed in July that year by the second two-seat prototype, the Ye-6U/2. It featured a balance weight of some 40kg, installed in the centrebody, next to frame 2, in order to improve the lateral stability and also boasted an increased internal fuel capacity of 2,340 litres. The vastly improved KAP-2 autopilot had altitude and speed correction functions. The SOD-57 air traffic control transponder was also added to the two-seater's avionics suite.

The two-seater's state testing programme, carried out by the NII-VVS, proved to be a very quick and straightforward undertaking. The concluding flight-test report, approved by the Soviet Air Force commander-in-chief in August 1961, noted that the two-seater sported the same manoeuvrability, stability and controllability as that of the MiG-21F-13 and the MiG-21PF, but also retained the chief shortcoming of high rudder forces at speeds in excess of Mach 1.4, making the aircraft's handling more difficult. The MiG-21U was cleared for operations from Class 2 paved runways no shorter than 2,000m. The NII-VVS test team also recommended in its final report that the MiG-21U's design should be further improved by adding the new SK-3 (KM-1) ejection seats, a KAP-3 three-axis autopilot and the SPS blown flaps system for reducing the landing speed.

The MiG-21UM is the definitive two-seat version of the MiG-21. This late-series example, seen at take-off, belongs to the former East German Air Force. (Author's collection)

In 1962 the MiG-21U two-seater entered series production at GAZ-31 in Tbilisi under the internal designation Type 66, while the NATO codename assigned was Mongol-A. The first three production-standard examples were rolled out in 1960 and as many as 180 MiG-21Us were produced at GAZ-31 between 1962 and 1966. A number of these aircraft (beginning with the seventh example of the sixth production batch) were built with the SPS blown flaps system, but they never achieved operational status as all the aircraft built at GAZ-31 retained the old R11F-300 engine, which lacked the bleed air capability. During the production run the MiG-21U's design was improved by the addition of an under-rudder brake parachute housing and an enlarged-area fin.

A view of the forward cockpit (left) and the rear cockpit (right) of a late-series MiG-21UM (Author)

The MiG-21U was also produced at GAZ-30 in Moscow for export customers between 1964 and 1968, with no fewer than 230 examples being built. A significant proportion of these featured the improved airframe design with the enlarged-area fin and parachute housing at the base of the fin.

The MiG-21US (Type 68; NATO codename: Mongol-B) was an improved two-seater derivative, sporting a number of novelties already implemented in the design of the MiG-21PFM. It was powered by the uprated R-11F2S-300 engine and featured the SPS blown flaps system; it also introduced KM-1M ejection seats (designated as the KM-1U

M-21/M-21M TARGET DRONES

In the 1980s a large number of surplus MiG-21PF/PFM/Rs were converted as full-scale aerial target drones to be used for trials and evaluation of new-generation AAMs and weapons control systems, receiving the designations M-21 and M-21M. The former was non-manoeuvring, while the latter version was a remotely piloted manoeuvring drone, used by the NII-VVS at its Akhtubinsk base in the southern part of Russia. All the development work related to the MiG-21's conversion into a drone was undertaken by the design bureau of the Kazan Aviation Institute, together with the Flight Research Institute of the Soviet Ministry of Aircraft Industry. The series conversion into drones was launched at the Soviet Air Force's own aviation repair plant at Lvov, in today's Ukraine. As many as 150 MiG-21PF/PFMs were produced there between 1985 and 2004.

The drone conversion necessitated removal of the Fishbed's radar, gunsight and some other mission equipment, while incorporating a set of new mission-specific equipment such as an automatic flight-control system with the AP-17 three-axis autopilot and actuators for the control surfaces and engine throttle, as well as a chaff/flare dispenser unit, a miss-distance indicator, equipment for flight path tracking from a ground station and a high-intensity flare for daylight visual tracking. After conversion, the M-21 and M-21M drones were flight-checked by test pilots before being declared fit for use in the unmanned mode.

Both the M-21 and M-21M were made capable of taking-off from both paved and non-paved runways, and were used for various test and evaluation programmes at the large shooting range near Akhtubinsk. Their maximum take-off weight was limited to 7,750kg, while flight profiles called for the drones to fly at altitudes between 50 and 14,400m (165 and 47,200ft). The maximum level speed at 10,000m (32,800ft) was limited to 1,800km/h, while the maximum flight endurance reached 1 hour 48 minutes. Maximum range was 1,000km. In order to evaluate the manoeuvring performance of the new-generation AAMs and air-intercept radars against manoeuvring targets, the M-21M was able to operate at up to 8.5G in the vertical and horizontal planes.

for the front and the KM-1I for the rear cockpit), a further improved KAP-2 autopilot and the definitive increased-area fin, 5.32m² in area. The MiG-21US also boasted an increased fuel capacity of 2,450 litres and had a brake parachute container at the base of the fin. The instructor's canopy received a periscope on a metal top rail in a bid to improve the view forward during take-off and landing: its upper mirror was automatically raised when the landing gear was extended and retracted with the retraction of the landing gear.

The MiG-21US prototype was flight-tested for the first time in 1965, and in 1966 it superseded the MiG-21U on the GAZ-31 production line in Tbilisi, with as many as 347 examples produced there until 1971.

The MiG-21UM (Type 69), known to NATO as the Mongol-C, was the definitive two-seater derivative of the type. It retained the basic airframe and systems design of the MiG-21US, but incorporated the uprated R-13-300 engine, although a number of early production examples retained the R-11F2S-300. It also introduced an entirely new flight/nav equipment suite, borrowed from the MiG-21S, including the AP-155 three-axis full-authority autopilot and the ASP-PFD-21 gunsight, while the equipment in the nose bay was installed in an easily removable rack.

Externally, the MiG-21UM can be distinguished from its predecessor by the presence of a DUA-3A AoA sensor on the port side of the nose (installed

 MIG-21 PROFILES

1. The MiG-21F prototype Ye-6/3 took to the air for the first time in December 1958 and was the first member of the MiG-21 family to introduce yaw vanes on the pitot boom, the SRO-2 Khrom IFF transponder, as well as a 490-litre centreline drop tank.
2. The Soviet Air Force MiG-21Rs operated in Afghanistan were grouped in the 263rd ORAE. This reconnaissance squadron, established in June 1980, was directly assigned to the 4th Army HQ. The squadron continued operations with the MiG-21R from Kabul until 1983, flying both reconnaissance and ground-attack missions.
3. This Egyptian Air Force MiG-21UM two-seater, seen in the early 2010s, wears a colourful livery used for dissimilar air combat training.
4. A Libyan Air Force MiG-21bis fighter involved in armed surveillance missions in 2012 and 2013 along the country's southern and eastern borders, preventing drug and arms trafficking and the influx of illegal immigrants.

1

2

3

4

for the first time in 1972). Some aircraft also featured a large blade antenna on the top fuselage, just in front of the fin, used by the ARK-10 ADF.

The MiG-21UM took to the air for the first time in 1968 and remained in production at GAZ-31 in Tbilisi between 1971 and 1985, with as many as 1,133 examples rolling off the line in 15 years.

OPERATIONAL HISTORY

The Indo–Pakistan wars

The MiG-21 saw its baptism of fire in the war between India and Pakistan in September 1965. Eight serviceable Indian Air Force MiG-21F-13s, equipping 28 Squadron, were used to fly combat air patrols (CAPs), in the vicinity of two forward Pakistan Air Force (PAF) airfields in Punjab, but no air-to-air combats were reported. The type had more contact during the next war with Pakistan, in December 1971. Equipping eight Indian Air Force squadrons at the time, the Fishbed saw active use in both the air-to-air and air-to-ground roles. There were a few air combats involving the MiG-21, the first of these taking place on 6 December, when a MiG-21FL shot down an F-6 attack aircraft, using the GP-9 gun-pod. On 12 December, during the first-ever reported clash between supersonic fighters, Indian MiG-21FLs managed to gun down a Pakistani F-104A Starfighter, again using the GP-9 gun-pod. On the last day of the war, 17 December, four more F-104As were claimed in air combats with the MiG-21FL, all of these on the account of 29 Squadron, without any losses of their own. The Fishbed also saw effective use in the air-to-ground role on the Eastern Front over what is now Bangladesh, employing a wide variety of weapons such as 500kg high-explosive bombs, napalm canisters, and S-24 240mm and S-5 57mm rockets, while the escorting MiG-21FLs were each armed with a pair of R-3S AAMs and a GP-9 gun-pod. The 500kg bombs were used to good effect by, for instance, a four-ship MiG-21 flight to inflict heavy damage on the runway of Tejadon Air Base near Dhaka. There was one MiG-21 air combat loss that occurred during a combat with Pakistani F-86F Sabres, while several Fishbeds returned to base with combat damage inflicted by the Pakistani anti-aircraft artillery (AAA).

The Fishbed in Indian service saw active use in the ground-attack role during the Kargil War with Pakistan in May–July 1999, supporting ground troops in high-altitude warfare in the Kargil district in the state of Kashmir. On 27 May 1999, one MiG-21bis was downed by a FIM-92 Stinger shoulder-launched surface-to-air missile (SAM) fired by Pakistani troops, while searching for the pilot of a MiG-27ML fighter-bomber who had ejected over the battle area due to engine failure. The Indian MiG-21 force also saw combat action shortly after the end of the Kargil War, downing a Pakistan Naval Air Arm Bréguet Atlantic maritime patrol aircraft with 16 crew on board. This incident occurred during an alleged violation of Indian airspace on 10 August 1999, with the MiG-21bis firing one R-60 missile that exploded next to the port engine; shortly after the hit, the stricken and burning Atlantic struck the ground, killing all onboard.

The Vietnam War

The MiG-21 was introduced into service with the Vietnamese People's Air Force (VPAF) in mid-1965. The type equipped one squadron of the 921st Fighter

Regiment (FR) at Noi Bai, which initially had a mixture of MiG-21PFs and MiG-21F-13s. The first use in anger of the type was reported in February 1966 and the first aerial victory was scored the following month, gunning-down a Ryan AQM-34 Firebee reconnaissance drone flying at 18,000m (59,000ft).

In April–May 1966, according to Soviet sources citing the recollections of the VPAF's Soviet military adviser Colonel Vladimir Babich, only RS-2US AAMs were employed by the VPAF MiG-21PFs in attacks against US aircraft, but reportedly without any success due to the very tight G-load manoeuvring restrictions and design deficiencies of the radar-beam guided missile. As many as 14 RS-2US missiles are said to have been launched in combat, all of which reportedly failed to hit their intended targets. The S-5 57mm rocket was another air-to-air weapon used in combat by the VPAF MiG-21F-13s and MiG-21PFs in 1965 and early 1966 because R-3S heat-seeking missiles had yet to be delivered.

The first R-3S heat-seeking missiles were delivered in April–May 1966, but their initial supply was very limited and as a consequence only the pair leaders were armed with them, while wingmen retained the two 16-round 57mm rocket packs. It necessitated that the first attack would be undertaken by the wingman with his rockets before the leader with his guided missiles. The first occasion on which this new tactic was employed was on 7 May 1966, when a pair of VPAF Fishbeds attacked an F-105 Thunderchief formation at low altitude. One Thunderchief was hit by an S-5 rocket, but subsequently managed to escape further attacks and returned to base. The first VPAF Fishbed victory against US manned aircraft was reported on 5 June 1966, when two F-4 Phantom IIs were downed by R-3S missiles. The VPAF's first MiG-21 combat loss was reported on 26 April 1966, when an aircraft was downed by an F-4 using air-to-air missiles, and the second Fishbed loss followed on 14 July 1966.

The most practical MiG-21 tactics devised by the VPAF, with assistance from Soviet advisers, called for the use of hit-and-run attacks, breaking at high speed through the fighter escort and attacking the strikers, forcing them to drop their bombs en route to their intended target. The VPAF had between 20 and 30 operational MiG-21s in 1966 and 1967, and the preferred method of their combat employment called for launching one or two pairs, vectored by GCI, to intercept from behind

FISHBED VS. B-52 IN *LINEBACKER I & II*

On 10 May 1972 Operation *Linebacker I* was launched, with sustained mass bombings by USAF and USN aircraft against important military, infrastructural and industrial targets north of the 20th Parallel. The small VPAF fighter force was stretched to the limit trying to counter the large-scale bombing raids, and faced stiff resistance from US fighters employing improved air combat tactics. In the spring and early summer months of 1972, the VPAF continued to suffer numerous and painful losses in air combat and also due to the heavy bombing of its ground infrastructure.

Despite the significant losses, the VPAF fighter force retained basic operating capabilities and the service commenced training a dozen Fishbed pilots in night intercept tactics, to challenge the B-52 Stratofortresses' bombing of targets in the north. There were, however, no chances to intercept a B-52 during Operation *Linebacker I*, as it was stopped on 22 October 1972 by US President Richard Nixon. Operation *Linebacker II*, which commenced on 17 December 1972, saw a resumption of the bombing campaign, in an attempt by President Nixon to force North Vietnam back to peace talks.

The bombings hit all the main VPAF airfields and a number of industrial centres, with B-52s heading for targets in the Hanoi area. An attempt by the MiG-21s to engage the B-52s took place on 18 December, when VPAF pilot Pham Tuan scrambled but failed to make contact with the enemy. On 27 December the same pilot was lucky at last, reportedly managing to penetrate the F-4 fighter escort and reach a three-strong bomber formation. The MiG-21MF was flying at 1,200km/h at 10,000m (32,800ft) as Tuan launched two R-3S heat-seeking missiles in salvo against one of the B-52s from 2,000m distance and immediately disengaged, breaking sharply and entering into a steep dive. The bomber was confirmed as a loss by the USAF, although it denied that the B-52 was downed by a Vietnamese MiG-21 and instead claimed that the loss was caused by a SAM hit. The second B-52 victory claimed by the VPAF was reported on 28 December, when pilot Vu Xuan Thieu managed to break through the American fighter escort and unleash his missiles, but his aircraft was lost and he died. It was guessed by Soviet military advisers, who examined the aircraft wreckage, that the MiG-21MF had rammed the B-52, while another version of events says that the fighter took hits from debris falling off the exploding bomber.

A classic propaganda photo depicting a trio of prominent VPAF fighter pilots in front of a row of MiG-21PF/PFMs armed with R-3S missiles; on the right is the VPAF's top ace Nguen Van Coc, who scored nine kills. (Author's collection)

US formations flying on known routes. So small and fast was the Fishbed that its pilots were able to mount often unseen high-speed attacks on the US Air Force (USAF) and US Navy (USN) integrated strike packages of fighter-bombers and escorting F-4s, heading to targets around Hanoi and Haiphong.

The year 1967 was a very difficult time for the VPAF's small Fishbed community, as five aircraft were lost during Operation *Bolo*, a large-scale counter-air operation launched by the USAF. A total of seven kills were claimed by the USAF, but VPAF and Soviet data confirmed only five losses sustained on 2 January 1967. Two days later, two more Fishbeds were reported to have been downed by USAF F-4s, with one pilot ejecting and another one killed.

After this heavy blow the VPAF Fishbed force was immediately grounded, but resumed combat operations four months later, adopting more effective hit-and-run tactics, preferably with high-speed attacks from the rear and above, followed by a prompt exit from the attack. The updated tactics were used for the first time on 31 April 1967, with two Fishbed pairs managing to down a total of four F-105s. A week earlier, however, a MiG-21 loss was reported in air combat with USAF F-4Cs.

November and December 1967 continued to be rather busy months for the VPAF Fishbeds, and the list of Vietnamese claims for the period comprised an RB-66 EW aircraft downed on 19 November (this claim was not confirmed by official US war losses records) an F-105 on 12 December and six days later three more F-105s from a formation approaching Hanoi. The only F-102A Delta Dagger loss was reported by the USAF on 3 February 1968; it turned out that this aircraft was downed by the top VPAF ace, Nguen Van Coc. Four days later, the same pilot downed a USN F-4B, this being his eighth kill of the war.

Between 1969 and 1971 there were no air-to-air combats over North Vietnam, following the Americans' unilateral cessation of all bombing operations, effective from 1 November 1968. There were, however, frequent intercepts of AQM-34 Firebee recce drones, with the VPAF claiming 10 in 1970 and one in 1971. In addition, there were some sporadic clashes in the air north of the 20th Parallel in 1970, with one F-4 (not confirmed by US war loss records) and one HH-53B Combat SAR helicopter claimed by the VPAF Fishbed force on 28 January; one MiG-21 was also reported lost in combat on that day.

A new phase of the war in early 1972 began with no success for the VPAF Fishbed community, as the type amassed painful losses but no victories at all until late April. By that time, the VPAF had two Fishbed fighter regiments – the 921st FR, equipped with the MiG-21MF (delivered in 1969), and the newly formed 927th FR, equipped with the older MiG-21PF and PFM interceptors.

Comparing the F-4 with the MiG-21 in manoeuvring air combat, Soviet military advisers assigned to the VPAF arrived at the conclusion that the US fighter boasted better acceleration and turning abilities in the vertical plane. However, F-4 pilots were instructed to engage in dogfights with the MiG-21 by performing manoeuvres in the horizontal plane and to avoid any vertical manoeuvring, as it was believed that the F-4 was superior at low altitude but that the MiG-21 had an edge in combat at medium and high altitudes.

The MiG-21's preferred air-to-air combat tactics when facing the F-4 in Vietnam were primarily influenced by the R-3S missile's minimum launch range of around 1,000m at medium/high altitude and the type's restricted manoeuvrability, imposed by the missile's 2G and 1.4G launch limitation at low/medium and high altitudes respectively. The R-3S was only capable of hitting targets manoeuvring at up to 3G, so by pulling harder, US fighter pilots had ample chances to escape from the missiles launched at them.

According to Soviet Air Force Major-General Mikhail Fesenko, who worked as military adviser to the VPAF commander-in-chief, in 1972 the North Vietnamese Fishbed force amassed 540 combat missions and suffered 34 losses, while the total number of victory claims, scored together with the MiG-17 and MiG-19 fleets, accounted for 89 US aircraft downed in the course of 201 air combats.

It is also noteworthy that there was a considerable difference between the kill claims of the warring parties. For instance, the VPAF kill claims list, as cited by prominent VPAF wartime operations researcher, Dr Istvan Toperczer, comprised of no fewer than 320 US aircraft, with 134 own losses admitted in air combats. In contrast, US claims (as per the US Navy official study) comprised 193 kills and 91 own losses or probable losses (six of these losses were on account of Chinese fighters that downed US aircraft after the latter had strayed into Chinese airspace). At the same time, there were some 22 aircraft in official US losses list for which no VPAF claims have been made at all. In the event, only 64 US losses were confirmed by both warring parties.

MiG-21s in the Arab–Israeli wars

The Fishbed entered service with the Egyptian Air Force (at the time known as the United Arab Republic Air Force) in 1963 and by the middle of the decade the fleet numbered about 60 MiG-21F-13s, supplemented not long after by 45–50 MiG-21PFs. The Syrian Air Force received its first MiG-21F-13s in 1961 and by 1966 it operated some 45 Fishbeds. In 1965 the radar-equipped MiG-21PF was inducted into Syrian service, with an initial batch comprising 15 examples plus six to eight two-seaters for use by both the F-13 and PF-equipped squadrons. The Iraqi Air Force was the third Arab air arm to receive the then-modern Fishbed, with around 60 MiG-21F-13s delivered between 1963 and 1966, together with some 60 MiG-21PFs and a few MiG-21U two-seat trainers. The Iraqi Fishbeds were the first of the type in the Arab world to see use in anger, flying a number of ground-attack sorties against Kurdish separatists in the northern and eastern parts of the country.

The Syrian MiG-21s' first use in anger dated from April 1967, as the type participated in a series of air combats against Israeli Air Force (IAF) fighters, reporting six losses and no victories at all in the initial encounters. In fact, this series of battles proved to be a prelude to an even more disastrous episode in the Fishbed's service in the Arab world, namely the Six-Day War in June 1967. It began with a sudden Israeli air attack against a number of Syrian, Egyptian

This Iraqi Air Force MiG-21F-13, wearing the serial '534', defected to Israel on 12 August 1966, flown by Captain Monir Radfa. (Author's collection)

and Iraqi airfields; the surprise attacks destroyed a large proportion of the Egyptian and Syrian MiG-21s on the ground. The success of the Israeli mass attack against the Egyptian forward airfields was undeniable; the Israeli jets faced very little resistance while mounting their devastating strikes on the first day of the war, 5 June 1967. A few MiG-21s that were able to take off to fight the attackers were promptly shot down, although a small number of surviving Egyptian MiG-21s were later used to attack the advancing Israeli ground forces, mostly deploying 57mm rockets. There were two composite Egyptian squadrons operating the MiG-21 during the war, in which all the survivors from the other air bases were gathered. One of the squadrons was stationed at Cairo West and flew air defence missions, while the other, operating from Inchas, was involved in air-to-ground missions.

The Syrian air arms had fewer than 20 fully operational Fishbeds at the onset of the Six-Day War, and a small proportion of these were used for escorting fighter-bombers and intercepting Israeli jets attacking Syrian airfields. No fewer than 18 aircraft (both operational and non-operational examples) were destroyed on the ground by the Israeli strikes during the first day. As a consequence only six Syrian Fishbeds are reported to have survived intact and continued fighting on 5 June and the following days.

The period between the Six-Day War and the October 1973 War (also known as the Yom Kippur War) saw a large number of clashes between fighters in the air, in which the Arab MiG-21s fought against Israeli jets with varying degrees of success. Egypt rapidly restored its Fishbed inventory thanks to a massive supply of new and second-hand aircraft from the Soviet Union, while Algeria also provided a number of MiG-21s. The first air combats over Sinai occurred barely one month after the end of the Six-Day War, and the first Israeli Mirage IIICJ was claimed on 15 July 1967, at the expense of two Egyptian MiG-21s reported lost in the same dogfight.

By the end of 1968 the Egyptian air arm already operated a fleet of about 115 MiG-21s, and not long after these Fishbeds were thrown into operations against Israel. The first large-scale air clash took place on 23 October 1968, with three Mirage IIICJs claimed by the Egyptians, although Israeli sources denied such losses. There were a good many air encounters in the following months, mostly in the form of interceptions of Israeli jets entering Egyptian territory at low level.

The official start of the so-called War of Attrition was announced by Egypt on 14 March 1969: it saw sporadic air and ground combat operations, aimed at inflicting damage on the Israeli defensive positions built alongside the western bank of the Suez Canal, and Egyptian aircraft took an active part in the attacks. Meanwhile, the improved MiG-21PFM entered Egyptian service at the beginning of 1969; it was the first radar-equipped interceptor version sporting the GP-9 gun-pod, a welcome complement to the R-3S missiles, useful at very close distances, less than 1,000m (3,300ft), where the R-3S was impossible to launch. In late 1969 the vastly improved MiG-21M with four missile launch rails and a GSh-23L built-in gun-pack was taken on strength.

At the same time, the Egyptians commenced training in new-style low-level interception and air combat tactics, in a bid to challenge the Israeli tactical superiority. In February and March 1970, 80 MiG-21MFs, sporting a more powerful engine and better radar, were delivered from the Soviet Union. In this new environment the clashes between the Israeli and Egyptian fighters continued, but with varying success for both parties. The biggest air battle from this period, where the Egyptian MiG-21s scored three widely publicized and acknowledged kills, took place on 11 September 1969. Two of these confirmed kills were Mirage IIIs, flown by prominent Israeli aces Giora Rom and Shlomo Weintraub, but five MiG-21s plus three other aircraft were lost in the same combat.

Soviet air combat data about the War of Attrition period showed that from July to December 1969, the United Arab Republic Air Force's losses were 72 combat aircraft, 53 of which were lost due to enemy action and a large proportion of which were MiG-21s. In total, the War of Attrition saw no fewer than 50 group air battles fought over both sides of the Suez Canal, claiming 60 Egyptian and 30 Israeli aircraft, according to Colonel Vladimir Babich. In turn, Israel admitted only four losses of its own in air combat – and only in those instances when the pilots were captured or found dead on Egyptian territory.

The onset of the 1973 October War saw the Egyptian air arm operating a fleet of about 200 MiG-21s of various versions and, just before the war, reinforcements from other Arab countries were taken on strength. In addition, Pakistani instructors and North Korean volunteers flew the MiG-21s in combat, while Algeria deployed to Egypt two squadrons, equipped with the MiG-21F-13 and MiG-21PF respectively. In addition to the air defence and escort missions, the Egyptian MiG-21s flew a large number of attack missions, armed with two 500kg or four 250kg bombs or 57mm rocket packs.

The war broke out on 6 October, with massive air attacks by the Egyptian Air Force, achieving tactical surprise and facing little opposition in the beginning. As a result, only one aircraft from the first wave was reported lost and by the end of the day the number of losses reached just ten jets. Next day, the IAF entered into decisive play, attacking the major Egyptian air bases in the Nile Delta. Massive air battles developed at low and medium altitudes as large numbers of Egyptian MiG-21s were scrambled to repulse the attack. On the second day, the MiG-21s continued flying attack sorties and the Algerian Fishbed force that had been deployed to Egypt saw combat for the first time.

The biggest air battle took place on 14 October, Day Nine of the war, as 62 MiG-21s stood against an Israeli attacking force of about 120 F-4E Phantom IIs and A-4 Skyhawks, launched in three waves against the large air base at al-Mansurah. In fact, this air battle proved to be the most successful action of the Egyptian air arm during the war and indeed its entire history, as it claimed no fewer than 20 victories at the expense of six losses of its own.

At the outbreak of the war, the Syrian air arm had on strength some 10 MiG-21 squadrons, the majority of them equipped with older Fishbed versions such as the F-13 and PF/PFM. The first Syrian war operations saw the MiG-21 flying escort missions for fighter-bomber formations launched in two waves to attack the Israeli positions. During the second wave of Day One, the first air clashes took place. At the same time, the IAF launched a counteroffensive aimed at destroying the Syrian SAM sites; this proved to be a failure and MiG-21s on CAP also assisted in repelling an F-4E anti-SAM attack, claiming two Israeli jets and reporting two own losses. In total, 12 Israeli jets were claimed on the second day of the war by the Syrians against 14 own losses.

A gun-camera sequence showing the destruction in the air of a United Arab Republic Air Force MiG-21, hit by 30mm rounds fired by an Israeli Mirage IIICJ fighter. (Author's collection)

Day Five of the war on the Syrian front saw 19 Israeli claims and 16 for the Syrians and Iraqis, and on this day the Syrian fighter force adopted the principal air defence responsibility over the frontline, since the surviving SAM units had run out of missiles. The same day, reinforcements from Iraq arrived in the form of 11 MiG-21MFs. The Israeli attacks against the Syrian airfields continued, with eight MiG-21s destroyed on the ground and one F-4E claimed by an Iraqi MiG-21 pilot. There were mass air battles fought over the frontline areas, with a number of Syrian MiG-21s claimed shot down while scoring only one victory, downing an A-4.

Day Six was even more difficult for the struggling Syrian fighter force and the Iraqis also continued to suffer painful losses, including at least two MiG-21s; they also claimed no fewer than four Israeli aircraft, but in fact only one or two were damaged in air combats and no kills were scored at all in the morning battles. Four more MiG-21s were downed in the afternoon of that hot day and another Iraqi Fishbed was lost to Syrian AAA.

The MiG-21 itself also suffered from a number of design shortcomings when employed in the low-altitude manoeuvring air combat role, as the type was never designed for such operations. In fact, when flown by skilled pilots, the Fishbed sported an impressive turning performance, especially when facing the Mirage III and F-4E. The improved training and better tactical skills were also among the major factors that contributed to the considerably increased kill ratio of the Egyptian and Syrian Fishbeds in the October War.

The next notable use of the MiG-21 in anger took place during the 1979 war between Egypt and Libya. The Egyptian Fishbeds were employed in the fighter-bomber escort role and clashed with Libyan Mirage V fighters, reporting one loss. In another air combat during that war, a pair of MiG-21MFs armed with AIM-9P Sidewinder missiles clashed with two Libyan MiG-23MS aircraft and gunned down one of the Floggers.

The Syrian MiG-21s were involved in a new series of air combats in July 1979, when the war between Israel and neighbouring Lebanon broke out. This time, however, the Syrians faced a vastly superior foe, as the IAF introduced both the F-15A Eagle and F-16A Fighting Falcon fourth-generation fighters. At that time, the Syrian air arm had a fleet of about 200 MiG-21s, most of them MFs, armed with the improved R-13M AAMs. The most fierce air battles before the full-scale war took place in May 1982, with no fewer than 20 MiG-21s lost. During the clashes before the June 1982 war in Lebanon, only one A-4 was claimed shot down by the Syrian Fishbeds. During the 1982 war, MiG-21 losses continued to mount due to the overwhelming Israeli superiority and poor Syrian tactics. On 9 June, during the famous Israeli air attack against the Syrian SAM batteries in the Bekaa Valley, no fewer than 10 MiG-21s were claimed in air combat, and another example was lost due to friendly fire. On 10 June 14 more MiG-21s were claimed lost in air combat;

E **MiG-21 VS F-4**

A VPAF MiG-21PFM belonging to the 927th Fighter Regiment, seen attacking a USAF F-4E fighter-bomber during Operation *Linebacker II*, July 1972. Supplies of new aircraft to North Vietnam by the Soviet Union in the late 1960s and early 1970s proved to be so massive that at all times the number of available MiG-21s was higher than the number of VPAF pilots trained on the type. A good many MiG-21PFMs were therefore placed in long-term storage. Such a resource eventually proved very useful in 1972, at a time of heavy attrition of aircraft due to the massed US air attacks against all known VPAF airfields.

the Fishbeds scored one kill only, downing an F-4E with cannon fire. On 11 June six more MiG-21s were lost in air combat, claiming another F-4E. This episode put an end to the MiG-21's use in the 1982 war.

Soviet MiG-21s in action

The prime MiG-21 operator in the 1960s and 1970s was the Soviet Air Force's Frontal Aviation branch, which had thousands of Fishbeds in frontline service, but the type saw little use in anger. Among the few instances when Soviet Fishbeds were employed in the air-to-air role during the Cold War era was the interception on 23 November 1973, when Captain Gennadii Yeliseev from the 982nd IAP (982nd Fighter Regiment), stationed at Vaziani airfield in the Soviet Republic of Georgia, downed an Iranian Air Force jet (believed to be a McDonnell Douglas F-4 fighter or Lockheed T-33 Shooting Star jet trainer) that had strayed into Soviet airspace. Initially, the MiG-21SM launched two R-3S missiles, which failed to hit the target. Since the distance between the interceptor and the target was too close for firing two more missiles and the Iranian jet was just about to cross the border line back into its own territory, Captain Yeliseev instead committed to ram the target, killing himself during the mid-air collision while the two crew members of the downed jet (an Iranian student pilot and a US instructor) managed to bail out safely.

At the beginning of the Soviet campaign in Afghanistan in 1979, the MiG-21 was the principal combat jet, with no fewer than 37 examples deployed to perform air defence and ground attacks. The 115th Guards IAP, a fighter regiment stationed at Kokaity in Uzbekistan, deployed to Bagram airfield on 27 December 1979 with one of its squadrons equipped with 12 MiG-21bis and two MiG-21UMs. The 136th APIB, a fighter-bomber regiment stationed at Chirchik in Uzbekistan and operating MiG-21PFMs, re-rolled as fighter-bombers, followed suit in early January 1980. Both of these units were reassigned to the 34th Air Corps, shortly afterwards transformed into the 40th Air Army, purposely established for operations in Afghanistan and headquartered at Bagram. In February 1980 another squadron drawn from the 115th Guards IAP was initially deployed to Bagram, but four months later it moved to Kandahar.

The 136th APIB was initially ordered to deploy its three squadrons to Kokaity and commenced flying its first patrols in Afghan airspace on 25 December 1979, with the aim of protecting the columns of Soviet ground forces entering the country. The principal area of operations for the fighter-bomber regiment covered the main roads used by the Soviet vehicle columns. Fishbeds flying these patrols were each armed with a pair of UB-32M rocket packs and also carried a centreline fuel tank. The fist combat sorties using weapons against the enemy forces on the ground were reported on 9 January 1980: a Soviet armoured vehicle and truck column fell under attack by Afghan *mujahedeen* fighters. The first air strikes were mounted by the quick-reaction alert (QRA) pair, scrambled from Kokaity, followed by a formation consisting of pilots from the regiment's command section. Each of the

A Soviet MiG-21bis from the 115th Guards IAP home-based at Kokaity in Uzbekistan. In addition to the first combat deployment in 1980–81, the regiment continued flying regular bombing missions against pre-planned targets in Afghanistan from its home airfield until 1989. (Author – *Aviatsia i Kosmonavtika*)

A selection of air-to-air and air-to-ground weapons displayed in front of this MiG-21bis pair, including UB-16-57 rocket packs and various missiles, while the aircraft nearest to the camera is armed with OFAB-100-120 high-explosive/fragmentation bombs. (Author)

Fishbeds unleashed 64 S-5 57mm rockets against *mujahedeen* fighters, who were on foot and mounted on horses.

One of the regiment's squadrons deployed to Kandahar in Afghanistan in early January 1980, while the second one was ordered to return home and undertake conversion to the more capable MiG-21SM; the third squadron remained at Kokaity for operations in the northern provinces of Afghanistan until the second half of February, when it too was ordered to deploy to Bagram. After its redeployment, this squadron immediately commenced flying attack sorties against a number of pre-planned targets such as opposition strongholds, with each MiG-21PFM using two 250kg high-explosive bombs. The 136th APIB continued operating the MiG-21SMs, re-rolled as fighter-bombers until April 1981; no combat losses were reported.

Due to the lack of significant air threats in Afghanistan, the two deployed fighter squadrons of the 115th Guards IAP were soon re-rolled in the ground-attack role, clashes with the *mujahedeen* having become more and more intensive in the months following the Soviet intervention, with the result that Soviet troops on the ground needed more and more air support. The main ground-attack weapons used by the MiG-21bis in the early stages of the war in Afghanistan were the OFAB-250-270 250kg high-explosive/fragmentation bombs, up to four per aircraft, most often dropped from steep 60° dive in two passes by using the MiG-21bis' ASP-PFD-21 gunsight in manual mode.

The workload on the Soviet MiG-21s in Afghanistan was pretty high, with 200–250 hours' annual utilization per aircraft, which translated to 400–450 sorties, most of them dedicated to real-world ground attacks. The simple and robust MiG-21, which lacked sophisticated avionics and systems, demonstrated good reliability in austere wartime operating conditions, and the fleet availability rate (represented by the percentage of combat-ready aircraft) was maintained at between 85 and 90 per cent.

The 115th IAP suffered two combat losses and saw the end of its combat deployment in Afghanistan in June 1981. Its three squadrons were replaced by two squadrons drawn from the 27th Guards IAP, home-based at Uch-Aral in Kazakhstan, each with 16 to 18 aircraft, including several two-seaters. The new squadrons were deployed to Bagram and Kandahar, and on 15 June 1981 the 27th Guards IAP reported its first combat loss: a MiG-21UM two-seater was shot down in the then (and now) notorious Tora-Bora cave area in the mountains next to the border with Pakistan. The aircraft was downed when flying at low altitude, killing one of the pilots, while the other crew member ejected and was captured on the ground, then sent to Pakistan and subsequently released. A second loss occurred shortly after the first one – the pilot managed to eject and was promptly rescued. The third loss during the regiment's combat deployment took place on 27 May 1982 – a MiG-21bis exploded in the air during an attack diving run (most likely hit by anti-aircraft fire from the ground), killing the pilot.

The next Soviet MiG-21 unit rotating through Afghanistan was the 145th IAP, home-based at Ivano-Frankovsk (now in the Ukraine). It commenced its one year-long combat deployment with two squadrons in mid-June 1982, stationed at Bagram and Kandahar, while a four-ship QRA flight was kept at Shindand in the southern part of the country. The deployment judged itself as lucky because the 145th IAP suffered no pilot losses during its 13 months of virtually non-stop combat operations and thousands of ground-attack combat sorties; only one MiG-21bis was reported downed near Bagram on 18 August 1982, but the pilot ejected and was quickly rescued.

The 927th IAP, home-based at Beryoza in Byelorussia, was the last Soviet Fishbed fighter unit deployed to Afghanistan. A two-squadron fleet of 28 single-seaters and four two-seaters arrived in theatre in late June 1983. After four days of joint operations with their predecessors, the 927th IAP commenced its independent combat work, amassing on average three to four combat sorties per aircraft each day. The bombing missions were usually flown by 8–12-ship groups, in order to ensure reliable destruction of the targets. The formations featured mixed ordnance loads, most often represented by the OFAB-250-270 bombs, S-24 rockets or UB-32M rocket packs. The 927th IAP's intense combat work saw some 10,000 sorties and 12,000 flying hours amassed during its 12-month Afghanistan deployment, lasting from June 1983 to June 1984. Each MiG-21bis logged around 400 hours, while pilots each had 250 to 400 combat hours under their belts. Combat losses accounted for two aircraft.

The 115th IAP, having moved back to Kokaity in Uzbekistan, only 50km from the border with Afghanistan, continued flying combat sorties from its home base on an occasional basis after its withdrawal from Afghanistan in mid-1981. From time to time it received orders to pound targets situated in the northern provinces of Afghanistan, and continued flying this type of combat mission until 1989. The MiG-21bis operating from the home base typically carrying one 800-litre centreline drop tank and were armed with two 500kg or four 250kg high-

The MiG-21 had a great career with the Soviet Air Force, serving in the advanced and lead-in fighter training role between the late 1960s and early 1990s. (Author – *Aviatsia i Kosmonavtika*)

explosive bombs. Due to the *mujahedeen* air defence, now considerably strengthened with more Stingers and 20mm AAA, all dive attacks commenced from 8,000m (26,200ft), with bombs released at 5,000m (16,400ft), followed by an immediate pull-out and climb with a minimum safe altitude of 3,000m (9,840ft) above ground level in order to avoid ground fire.

The Soviet MiG-21Rs permanently based in Afghanistan were used for both reconnaissance and ground-attack missions in the war theatre. Initially it was a squadron drawn from the 87th ORAP, an independent reconnaissance regiment stationed at Karshi in Uzbekistan, which deployed to Bagram in January 1980 with ten MiG-21Rs. In April the same year it was promptly replaced by the 229th OAETR, an independent reconnaissance squadron, home-based at Chortkov in the Ukraine. In June 1980, the squadron was moved to Kabul, where the permanent 263rd ORAE was established, directly assigned to the 40th Air Army HQ. It continued operations from Kabul until 1983, with air and ground crews drawn from a number of Soviet Air Force reconnaissance regiments and deployed on a rotational basis for one year. The 263rd ORAE's main activity involved taking photographs of areas of interest, situated all over the war-torn country, such as important mountain passes and areas controlled by the armed opposition, as well as locations of expected large-scale combat operations to suppress the armed opposition. The MiG-21Rs were also used for post-strike reconnaissance missions.

During the first year of the war as many as 2,708 combat sorties were flown by the crews of the 263rd ORAE, and between January and December 1980 as many as 607 ELINT sorties were logged, initially by the MiG-21Rs of 87th ORAP and from April by the 263rd ORAE. When used in the ground-attack role, the MiG-21R was armed mainly with 250kg and 500kg free-fall bombs, ZAB-360 napalm canisters and occasionally 57mm rockets for area saturation. As veteran pilot Alexander Bondarenko, who flew with the 263rd ORAE in 1981, recalled, the Fishbed-H fared well and proved suitably flexible and agile for both the recce and attack missions in the specific Afghan conditions. Between 1980 and early 1983 the 263rd ORAE reported five MiG-21Rs and four pilots lost in action. The Fishbed-H remained in use with the squadron until April 1983, when it was replaced by the Su-17M3R.

Iraqi MiG-21s in combat

By 1980 the Iraqi Air Force/Air Defence Force operated some 90 MiG-21MFs, plus a handful of MiG-21F-13s and two-seaters, serving with five fighter squadrons, as well as a small number of MiG-21Rs. During the war with Iran, the MiG-21 was pitted against the technologically superior F-4D Phantom II and F-14A Tomcat, while the nimble F-5E Tiger II was regarded as a less serious opponent. The only chance the Iraqi MiG-21 pilots had when fighting against the F-4 and F-14 was if they enjoyed the element of surprise in close encounters – but this proved to be a very rare occurrence.

Even before the war, on 10 September 1980, two MiG-21Rs were lost while on a reconnaissance mission inside Iranian airspace, downed by an F-14A, and four days later four more Fishbeds, also flying over Iranian territory, were gunned down by F-4s. After war broke out on 22 September 1980, Iraqi losses continued to mount, with three Fishbeds claimed by the Iranian fighter force on the first day, while the second day of the war saw Iraqi MiG-21s claiming two F-5Es. At the beginning of the war, Iraqi MiG-21s also flew low-level attack missions against ground targets, most often armed with 250kg general-purpose bombs.

During the flowing phases of the war, the MiG-21 was mainly used as a point-defence interceptor, tasked to protect the capital Baghdad and the northern part of the country from the attacks of Iranian fighter-bombers. In early 1981 the Iraqi MiG-21s received considerably better air-to-air weapons in the form of the French MATRA Magic Mk 1 heat-seeking missile, and became operational with this weapon in March 1981. The new missile replaced the rather antiquated R-3S and proved more successful in combat. Within one week in May 1981, two F-4Es, two F-5Es and one AH-1J Cobra attack helicopter were claimed by the Iraqis, who lost only one MiG-21; soon afterwards, two more F-4s and F-5s were claimed shot down, using the Magic Mk 1 missiles. The Iraqi MiG-21s also used AIM-9B Sidewinder AAMs obtained from Jordan in 1983, managing to shot down with this new weapon two F-5s, one F-4D, one C-130H Hercules transport aircraft and a Bell 214 helicopter.

In 1983 the Iraqi MiG-21 inventory was reinforced with the arrival of some 40 Chinese-made F-7Bs, obtained with the help of Saudi funding. A batch of 25 MiG-21bis was also taken on strength in the same year, followed not long after by another batch of the same Fishbed derivative, already armed with the R-60 agile dogfight missile. In fact, the Iraqi Fishbed fleet continued operating until the end of the war; but the type was rapidly overshadowed by more capable and longer-legged fighters, such as the MiG-23 and Mirage F1, and had few further successes in combat, such as downing an AH-1J Cobra in October 1983.

The Iraqi inventory of some 120 MiG-21s and F-7Bs failed to have any impact during the 1990–91 Gulf War. The only known instance of air combat occurred on 17 January 1991, with four MiG-21s acting as decoys to divert an F-14A combat air patrol, while two more Fishbeds attempted to attack an F/A-18A Hornet formation from USS *Saratoga*, launched on a mission against the H-3 airfield complex in the western part of Iraq. The attacking MiG-21 pair, however, had the bad luck of flying directly into the main strike package and consequently both the Fishbeds were immediately shot down by the Hornets.

MiG-21s in the former Yugoslavia

The Yugoslavian Air Force had a fleet of no fewer than 160 active MiG-21s by 1991, when the Yugoslavian Federation commenced its bloody break-up. The majority of the Fishbeds were the MiG-21bis version, accounting for some 80 examples, as well as 40 MiG-21M/PFMs and a dozen MiG-21R/MFs used in the recce role, plus about two dozen of the two-seaters.

During the civil war in the first half of the 1990s, the Yugoslavian MiG-21bis force was used to fly close air support (CAS) and occasional battlefield interdiction missions, initially in Slovenia from 28 June to 2 July 1991, and then in Croatia and Bosnia. The number of combat sorties over the Croatian region of eastern Slavonia in 1991 exceeded 550. In the course of fighting to support the operations of the Yugoslavian federal armed forces in the breakaway Croatia, three MiG-21bis and one MiG-21R were shot down by ground fire. A MiG-21R with a Croatian pilot, Captain 1st Class Rudolf Peresin, defected to Klagenfurt in Austria in October 1991, and three more pilots defected to airfields in Croatia (see below).

The Yugoslavian MiG-21bis scored one aerial victory during the war – it happened on 7 January 1992 in north-western Croatia near Novi Marof. The victim, which was gunned down with an R-60 missile, proved to be an Italian Army Aviation AB-205 transport helicopter, painted in all-white and used by the European Community Monitor Mission; four Italian officers and one

French officer were killed. A second AB-205 helicopter, flying with the downed one as a pair, was also attacked and made a crash-landing.

In 1992 all the federal MiG-21 units based in Croatia and Bosnia were withdrawn to Serbian territory and, in May 1992, the Yugoslavian MiG-21 force undertook its last action during the initial phase of the civil war, attacking a ferry crossing a river in northern Bosnia and apparently transporting Croatian soldiers. In the same month another MiG-21bis was downed by the Croats, becoming the seventh federal Fishbed to be lost in action since the outbreak of the war in June 1991.

The newly born Croatian Air Force got its first three MiG-21 fighters thanks to the defection of three pilots of Croatian nationality who were serving with the Yugoslavian Air Force. The first flew to Pula in Croatia in February 1992, while the second and third ones followed suit the following May. These Fishbeds, serialed 101 through 103, were quickly painted with Croatian insignia and pressed into action during the early days of the war in Bosnia in 1992–93. MiG-21bis 101, named *Avenger of Dubrovnik*, was lost in June 1992 and its pilot, Lieutenant-Colonel Antun Rados, was killed. MiG-21bis 103, named *Avenger of Vukovar*, was lost at Stipan in September 1993 during a four-ship mission attacking Serbian R-65 Luna tactical missile launchers; its pilot, Lieutenant-Colonel Miroslav Peris, was killed.

In 1994 a batch of about 40 MiG-21bis and UMs were covertly purchased by Croatia (due to the UN-imposed arms embargo) from the former Soviet republic of Ukraine. Some 25 of these second-hand Fishbeds were promptly restored to airworthy condition to equip two squadrons (the 21st stationed at Pleso near Zagreb and the 22nd at Pula), while the reminder were used for spares. Both the newly established squadrons were staffed by experienced pilots who had served with the Yugoslavian Air Force, most of them having a rich MiG-21 and MiG-29 background. To maintain secrecy about the number of MiG-21s in service, no visible serial numbers were applied in the initial years. Lieutenant Colonel Rudolf Peresin, the pilot who defected with a MiG-21R to Klagenfurt in Austria in 1991, became CO of the first squadron. He was killed in action on 2 May 1995, during Operation *Flash*, while on a CAS mission attacking targets in the Serb-held enclave in western Slavonia, flying MiG-21bis 119.

The most notable Croatian Fishbed operations during the Croatian War of Independence were carried out during the offensives aimed at recapturing the territories of western Slavonia in May 1995 (Operation *Flash*) and the large-scale offensive in the Serb enclave of Krajina, known as Operation *Storm*. The latter was conducted between 4 and 9 August 1995, with the main objective being to liberate areas held by the Serbs in south-central Croatia. Seventeen MiG-21bis and two UMs were available at the start of the battles. Thirteen MiG-21s were used on the first day of the operation, tasked to attack six targets; one of these suffered heavy damage and three more returned to base with light damage. On 5 August a communications facility was bombed by the Croatian Fishbeds, as well as a weapons storage facility and other targets in Krajina, and on 6 August a command post, a bridge and four other military targets came under attack. A MiG-21 pair was also used for CAP, but eventually failed to intercept Krajina Serb attack jets operating in the area against the Croatian ground forces.

On 7 August the Croatian MiG-21 force continued flying combat sorties, attacking Serb positions and tanks near Bosnanski Petrovac. On 8 August further attacks were mounted against tanks and armoured vehicles mixed with civilian vehicles, with two MiG-21s sustaining damage from anti-aircraft fire, while on the ground there were numerous military and civilian casualties.

In total, during Operation *Storm*, the Croatian Air Force conducted 200 sorties, including 67 for CAS, seven for reconnaissance and four for CAP sorties over the battlefield, while the others were described as air defence sorties.

During the Kosovo war in 1999, the Yugoslavian air arm had on strength some 26–30 combat-ready MiG-21s, but these by then hopelessly obsolete fighters were judged to have no chance of countering the mass air attacks mounted by the NATO forces. No combat missions were flown during the 1999 war and the Fishbed fleet was kept on ground alert in hardened shelters or camouflaged in dispersed locations. As many as 33 Yugoslavian Fishbeds – 25 MiG-21bis', two Ms and six UMs – were reported destroyed during the NATO bombing between March and June 1999, although all 12 aircraft (11 single-seaters and one two-seater) kept in the underground shelter at Pristina-Slatina airfield in Kosovo survived intact despite the frequent NATO attacks and several attempts to destroy their cave shelter. After the end of the war, all of these aircraft were promptly ferried to Batajnica near Belgrade.

CONCLUSION

The cone-nosed Fishbed occupies a prominent position in the aviation history of Russia/Soviet Union, as its most popular and successful jet fighter. It stayed in series production for 28 years, considerably longer than both its predecessor, the MiG-19, and successor, the MiG-23, with no fewer than 11,000 examples rolled out at three plants in the Soviet Union and three more plants situated abroad (Czechoslovakia, India and China). Furthermore, the MiG-21's latest non-licensed Chinese copies, sporting significant airframe and equipment improvements, continued in production for export to developing states until mid-2013.

The MiG-21's frontline career with the Soviet Air Force was a relatively short one, with its mass service lasting from the early 1960s to the mid-1970s, and the Fishbed was rapidly overshadowed in the late 1970s and early 1980s by several new and more capable frontline types, such as the MiG-23, MiG-29, Su-17 and Su-27. The small delta-winged fighter enjoyed a long and productive service in the advanced/lead-in training role, however, operated by no fewer than 30 Soviet Air Force training regiments between the late-1960s and early 1990s. The total fleet of these training units at the height of the Fishbed's career accounted for no fewer than 1,500 aircraft.

A short-legged fighter with austere mission equipment and an unimpressive warload, the MiG-21 was widely appreciated as a supersonic fighter that was easy both to maintain and fly. It eventually achieved huge export successes, used by all the Soviet-friendly states in the 1960s, 1970s and 1980s, as well as by a good number of non-aligned nations all around the world. No less than 3,000 examples were sold or supplied as military aid free of charge to about three dozen export customers, and a proportion of these Fishbeds remain in active service today. Furthermore, the MiG-21 family continues to be among

F **FISHBEDS IN THE BALKANS**
The Croatian Air Force conducted effective MiG-21 ground attack operations during Operation *Storm* in August 1995. The highly skilled pilots, who had served with the Yugoslavian Air Force until the break-up of the Yugoslavian Federation, proved instrumental for the efficiency of the combat use of the type, which used bombs and rockets with an impressive preciseness during the close air support and air interdiction missions.

A modern-day MiG-21 pilot patch; a reminder that the delta-winged fighter remains in active service worldwide. (Author)

the principal fighter types in most if not all of the countries considered rogue to the Western world, such as North Korea, Syria and Cuba, while Iran has a sizeable quantity of Chinese-built F-7s.

In the 21st century, a good many MiG-21s continued to be active worldwide, with the Indian fleet being the most numerous one and maintaining quite a high flight operations tempo, albeit with a poor flight safety record. The list of the other countries maintaining significant Fishbed fleets includes Vietnam and Egypt, while the type continues to serve as a NATO air defence asset with the air arms of Bulgaria, Romania and Croatia.

From the operational point of view, it is noteworthy that the Soviet Air Force and its Warsaw Pact allies placed great emphasis on utilizing the MiG-21's speed, especially as a medium-to-high level point-defence interceptor, tightly controlled by GCI, while low-speed manoeuvres were banned in the frontline units. As a consequence, the type's true manoeuvring capability and dogfighting potential in this corner of the envelope remained completely unknown to the Soviet and Warsaw Pact air arms throughout the entire service career of the Fishbed; but this otherwise little-known strength was, in fact, well-explored by some Arab operators as well as by the Indian Air Force. It is also the case that the low-speed manoeuvrability of the Fishbed in air combat was highly appreciated by US pilots serving with the secretive 'Red Eagles' squadron (officially referred to as the 4477th Test & Evaluation Squadron), which flew ex-Indonesian Air Force MiG-21F-13s in the 1970s and 1980s. The Red Eagles pilots, who had plenty of experience on the type flying as aggressors, free from the stringent operating/handling restrictions imposed on their Soviet counterparts, tended to describe the Fishbed-C's manoeuvring characteristics and slow-speed handling as both compelling and absolutely out of the ordinary. They claimed that the MiG-21 was forgiving to fly and well capable of performing manoeuvres that contemporary US aircraft could not, at least not without their engines stalling and flaming out.

The great career of the MiG-21 in mass operations worldwide is nearing its end, though there are a few operators, such as India, that are planning to continue flying the type until the late 2020s. (Author)

FURTHER READING

Books

Cooper, Tom and Weinetrt, Peter and Hinz, Fabian and Lepko, Mark, *African MiGs*, Vol 1 and Vol 2, Harpia Publishing (2010 & 2011)

Belyakov, Rostislav and Jaques Marmain, *MiG Aircraft 1939–1995* (in Russian), Aviko Press (1996)

Braybrook, Roy, 'The MiG-21 Fishbed', *Flying Review*, Vol 19, No 2, pp.20–22

Davies, Steve, *Red Eagles: America's Secret MiGs*, Osprey Publishing (2008)

Gordon, Yefim and Bill Gunston, *MiG-21 Fishbed*, Aerofax (1996)

Jane's All the World's Aircraft, 1976–1977, Jane's Publishing Company Limited (1976)

Lambert, Mark, 'Flying the Fishbed', *Flight International*, 25 September 1975, pp.443–44

Markovskii, Viktor, *Burnt Afghanistan Skies* (in Russian), Yauza Moscow (2012)

Mladenov, Alexander, 'Fishbeds in Bulgarian Service', *AIR International*, April and May 2001, pp.172–77 and 214–17

Nicolle, David and Tom Cooper, *Arab MiG-19 and MiG-21 Units in Combat*, Osprey Publishing (2004)

Toperczer, Istvan, *Air War Over North Vietnam*, Squadron/Signal Publications (1998)

Toperczer, Istvan, *MiG-21 Units of the Vietnam War*, Osprey Publishing (2001)

Yakubovich, Nikolai, *MiG-21 Birth of a Legend* (in Russian), Zeithouse (2007)

Yakubovich, Nikolai, *MiG-21 Interceptors and Reconnaissance Variants* (in Russian), Zeithouse (2007)

Yakubovich, Nikolai, *MiG-21 Last Variants* (in Russian), Zeithouse (2007)

Yakubovich, Nikolai, *MiG-21 Fighter 'Russian spirit' against Phantoms, Mirages and Thunderchiefs* (in Russian), Yauza/Elsmo (2012)

Documents

MiG-21F-13 Handling Technique & Combat Employment Methodology Guide, Part II, Combat Employment, (in Russian) Military Publishing House, Moscow (1963)

MiG-21R Aircraft: A version Technical Description, Supplement to MiG-21PFMA's Technical Description (in Russian), Moscow (1971)

MiG-21PFM (MiG-21PF) Pilot's Manual, Part 1 Flight Operations (in Russian) Moscor (1977)

MiG-21PF (MiG-21PFM) Aircraft Operating Manual (in Russian), Moscow (1980)

MiG-21R variant A, D & R pods technical description (in Russian), Sofia (reprint 1971)

INDEX